Options For Undergraduate Foreign Language Programs

Four-Year and Two-Year Colleges

Renate A. Schulz

407.1173
Sch80
113985
May 1980

This study was conducted with the support of the National
Endowment for the Humanities, Division of Education
Programs (Grant No. EH27125-77-67). Opinions expressed
are those of the author and do not reflect the views or
policies of the sponsoring agency.

Published by The Modern Language Association of America
62 Fifth Avenue, New York, New York 10011

CONTENTS

Each and every human tongue is a distinct window onto the world. Looking through it, the native speaker enters an emotional and spiritual space, a framework of memory, a promontory on tomorrow, which no other window in the great house at Babel quite matches. Thus every language mirrors and generates a possible world, an alternative reality.

By means of language human beings can do something utterly fantastic—they can say "No." "No" to what would otherwise be the seeming inevitability of organic life, the monotony of birth and death. Every single language contains a world, a rich world of human freedom, as against the inevitable organic world of our animal lives.

—George Steiner in "The Coming Universal Language," *The Listener* (London: BBC Weekly); reprinted in *Atlas World Press Review*, 24 (October 1977), pp. 24–26.

ACKNOWLEDGMENTS

This study came about through the cooperation and efforts of many individuals. Special thanks are due Dr. H. G. Moss, Assistant Director of Education Programs at the National Endowment for the Humanities, who was responsible for administering the grant that supported the research reported here. Thanks are also due the Modern Language Association, especially Mr. Richard Brod, for many suggestions and for providing access to the files of past enrollment surveys and the "1974–75 Survey of Non-Traditional Curricula."

I am indebted to my consultants for this project, Professors John B. Carroll (University of North Carolina), Kimberly Sparks (Middlebury College), and Edward D. Sullivan (Princeton University), for reacting both to the proposal and to the final report. I am especially grateful to a fourth consultant, Professor David P. Benseler (Ohio State University), for helping with the tabulation of results and for providing encouragement, critical comments, and numerous suggestions throughout the study.

I am also grateful to the following colleagues for reacting to the draft of the questionnaire that was used in the study: Professors Edward D. Allen (Ohio State University), Howard B. Altman (University of Louisville), J. Wayne Connor (University of Florida), Maurice W. Conner (University of Nebraska at Omaha), Don A. Dillman (Washington State University), Ernest A. Frechette (Florida State University), Gilbert A. Jarvis (Ohio State University), Robert C. Lafayette (Indiana University), Wilga M. Rivers (Harvard University), Neil Rudin (State University of New York-College at Buffalo), Jean-Charles Seigneuret (Washington State University), Lorraine Strasheim (Indiana University), and Sidney N. J. Zelson (State University of New York-College at Buffalo).

My thanks to the Research Foundation of the State University of New York (College at Buffalo) for handling the administrative details of the grant despite my move to another institution midstream during the study; to the

Foreign Language Department at State University College at Buffalo for releasing me from teaching duties to do the research; and to my department at the University of Arkansas for providing the encouragement, released-time, and secretarial assistance that enabled me to complete this report.

Above all, I am indebted to the many chairpersons who took the time to complete the questionnaire and whose comments, experiences, and insights provide the essence of this report. I am particularly grateful to the nineteen institutions that permitted me to take a firsthand look at their foreign language programs.

And finally, a special thank you to my daughter Sigrid for attempting to understand with eleven-year-old maturity why mother wasn't home on Halloween, Thanksgiving, and some other important days in her life.

Renate A. Schulz
University of Arkansas, Fayetteville
September 1978

INTRODUCTION

There are numerous reasons for Americans (or anyone else, for that matter) to learn a foreign language. Foreign language study is believed to sharpen analytical and intellectual skills, to lessen ethnocentricity, to enhance one's tolerance of the values and behavioral patterns of other cultural groups, and to increase awareness of the complexity of the communication process, of language in general, and of one's native tongue in particular. Knowing a foreign language can contribute to international understanding and, of course, enables an individual to communicate with people of another culture—either face-to-face or through written documents. Maria Alter provides thirty-six "traditional reasons" and five "modern" ones for requiring foreign language study, all valid for selected groups of the population.[1] Additional reasons are given by Dodge, Grittner, Honig and Brod, Jarvis, Lawson, Strasheim, and others.[2] Few would doubt that knowledge of a foreign language can be a valuable asset to virtually any individual or any profession; American business, industry, government, and social and cultural institutions need, more than ever, professionals with proficiency in at least one foreign language.

But despite a sound rationale supporting foreign language study, despite the fact that our government cosigned the Helsinki Agreement in 1975, pledging its active support and encouragement to furthering the study of foreign languages and civilizations on all levels, and despite presidential and gubernatorial proclamations of the importance of language study, foreign language enrollments at all levels of formal education have plummeted since the late sixties. Statistics compiled from institutions of higher learning by the Modern Language Association of America reflect an overall enrollment decrease of 21.2% between 1968 and 1977. In 1965, 17.6% of the students enrolled in postsecondary education studied a foreign language; by 1977, this percentage had dwindled to 8.9%.[3]

The decline in national enrollments certainly cannot be attributed to a lack of well-trained teachers (an estimated fifty-four percent of recent Ph.D.'s in foreign languages and literatures have not found positions in the fields for which they were trained)[4] or to professional apathy. Numerous conferences and publications dealing with professional concerns present a rich selection of program descriptions and curricular innovations, proposals, and critiques. (Of particular interest are the *ADFL Bulletin, Modern Language Journal, Foreign Language Annals*, the ACTFL Foreign Language Education Series, and the recently published *German Studies in the United States*,[5] as well as the journals published by the American Associations of Teachers of French, German, Italian, Slavic and East European Languages, and Spanish and Portuguese, and the American Classical League.) Generally speaking, reasons for the decline in interest in foreign language study lie outside the immediate control of foreign language departments. For instance, many educators agree that today's student is more pragmatic and career-oriented than were students of previous generations: In the words of one chairman, "students feel that if you can't do much with it after one semester, it ain't worth studying." And reaping the tangible benefits of foreign language study in terms of proficiency in a foreign language takes a long-term commitment of time and energy that only a small percentage of students are willing to make. Demands for immediate "relevance," protest against regimentation and uniformity, and emphasis on individual choice and "self-fulfillment," voiced frequently in the sixties, have done away with many of the traditional requirements formerly considered indispensable to the "mark of an educated man." Because of the size and self-sufficiency of the United States and because of the spread of English as *lingua franca* throughout the industrialized world, there is little pragmatic impetus toward foreign language study. Moreover, financial cutbacks in higher education have severely affected the relatively expensive (in terms of student/teacher ratio and library budgets) foreign language departments, relegating many departments with a small number of majors to a strictly "service" function.

What methods are successful in reversing the trend of falling enrollments in U.S. colleges and universities, and how can the proclaimed values of foreign language study benefit a larger proportion of the student population? These basic questions motivated the survey reported here, a study conducted with the support of the Division of Education Programs of the National Endowment for the Humanities.

The purpose of the study was to identify successful foreign language programs in undergraduate institutions of higher learning and to examine those factors that contributed to their success. Basically, a successful program was defined as one that attracted and maintained student interest and met its specifically stated objectives. In short, the study attempted to find patterns and approaches to foreign language instruction that might be generalized, reproduced, or adapted by other institutions to generate student interest and improve teaching and learning.

Since enrollment figures were the only objective measure available from a large number of institutions, the initial criterion for success was stated in terms of enrollment increases between the fall terms of 1972 and 1976. Admittedly, a predominantly quantitative criterion is open to criticism. Success in terms of numbers alone is suspect in education since students frequently choose a course (particularly if the course satisfies a requirement) because it is "the lesser of the evils" in terms of required work and effort. Ideally, program success should be measured both qualitatively and quantitatively—in terms of student learning as well as the ability of a program to generate student interest on all levels of instruction. Unfortunately, few departments have developed a unified set of objectives or collected systematic comparative data on student achievement. Even anecdotal accounts of student achievement related to particular approaches or methodologies are not always corroborated by the impressions of a majority of colleagues within a department.

"Innovation" cannot be considered a sole indicator of success since innovative or non-traditional approaches in themselves give no assurance of either qualitative or quantitative change in achievement or enrollment. Attempts to follow up some of the non-traditional courses or teaching approaches reported in the professional literature and particularly by the "Report on the 1974–75 Survey of Non-Traditional Curricula," conducted by the Modern Language Association,[6] revealed more often than not that the "innovation" ran out with the energy and emotional steam of the innovator and thus did not become an integral part of the curriculum. Moreover, much of the innovation and experimentation conducted in foreign languages, if it is maintained past the initial "Hawthorne effect" of almost any experimental effort, makes no attempt at evaluation. (It appears that too many educators "experiment" just long enough to get a professional publication out of their efforts—without systematic follow-up of the results of experimentation and innovation.)

A further justification of the quantitative criterion for success—from a pragmatic perspective—is that in most American institutions of higher education enrollment is the major criterion for administrative, and thus financial, support. Regardless of how innovative a course, or how successful in terms of student learning, if enrollment does not generate the minimally expected FTE's, most administrations consider the course economically unfeasible.

In order to survey as large a sample of American institutions as possible, a questionnaire was sent in February 1977 to all foreign language departments (or departments teaching foreign languages) in undergraduate four-year and two-year colleges. (See Appendix A for a copy of the questionnaire.) The computerized files of the Modern Language Association provided the address base. The initial mailing went to 3,288 departments, 964 of which were in community colleges. For the follow-up mailing, sent in early April, those departments (such as departments of comparative literature or linguistics in large universities) that did not engage in formal foreign language instruction were eliminated from the MLA mailing list, and questionnaires were sent a second time, with a new cover letter, to 3,140 departments. The cover letter for the second mailing had two forms, differentiating between institutions that showed a foreign language enrollment increase according to the MLA's 1974 enrollment survey and those that did not. (According to that survey, 577 of the total number of responding four-year institutions and 300 of responding two-year institutions indicated enrollment increases.)

The questionnaire requested data on undergraduate enrollment figures in the various languages taught at each institution for the autumn terms of 1972, 1974, and 1976, respectively. Figures for graduating majors and total institutional enrollments as well as for the number of teaching staff available to each department were requested for the same years. In addition, the questionnaire sought information on the foreign language requirement at each institution; the requirement on new courses or programs instituted in the department since the fall term of 1972; on the most popular courses (in terms of enrollment) past the introductory level; and on undergraduate curricular options, special methodological approaches, and evaluation practices. The questionnaire also requested a narrative statement on causes for the increase or decrease of enrollments in particular departments. Unfortunately, because of time constraints, pretesting the questionnaire by sending it to a random sample of chairpersons was impossible. A draft was sent, however, to twenty-two foreign language educators, researchers, and department chairpersons, as well as to several sociologists, and their suggestions were incorporated in the final questionnaire. The data obtained from responding departments were compiled, and quantitative summaries and averages were calculated when appropriate. The findings of the study are presented separately for four-year and two-year institutions in the following sections of this book.

From the responding departments, fifteen four-year institutions and four two-year institutions were selected for a follow-up study including on-site visitation. The following factors were considered in choosing departments for a more detailed study:

- increase in enrollments and/or majors since 1972, taking into account overall institutional growth (in multilanguage departments, those departments that showed increases in more than one language were favored for selection);
- no increase in foreign language requirements since 1972 (those institutions without formal requirements were given precedence);
- number and kind of new courses or programs developed since 1972 (a program was defined as two or more courses leading to a specified objective, e.g., a translator's certificate, a degree in international business, or a career-related course sequence);
- number of options or methodological approaches listed;
- additional information supplied in narrative form by respondents;
- distribution by region and size of institution, including public and private schools.

The following institutions were visited:

Public Four-Year Institutions

Ohio State University	(Classics)
Oregon State University	(German)
State University of New York– College at Buffalo	(Foreign Languages)
University of California at Berkeley	(French, Italian)
University of Maryland at College Park	(Spanish)
University of Michigan at Ann Arbor	(Romance Languages)
University of Northern Iowa	(Foreign Languages)
University of Oregon	(Spanish)
University of Texas at El Paso	(Foreign Languages)
Washington State University	(Foreign Languages)

Private Four-Year Institutions

Brown University   (Classics, Slavics, and Spanish)
Dartmouth College   (French, German, and Russian)
Middlebury College   (Foreign Languages, Summer Program)
Pomona College   (Foreign Languages)
University of Southern California   (Spanish)

Two-Year Institutions

Portland Community College-Sylvania Campus (Oregon)
San Antonio College
San Francisco City College
Tarrant County Junior College-Northeast Campus (Texas)

Visits to the various campuses lasted from one to three days and included both class visitation and conferences with chairpersons, program coordinators, a sampling of faculty members, teaching assistants (where involved in undergraduate instruction), students, and administrators.

Descriptive summaries of selected programs are presented in chapters iv and viii. Because of expense, time, and other factors, not all promising departments could be visited. This report is not, therefore, a conclusive summary of curricular trends. It is sincerely hoped, however, that the findings and curricular practices summarized here will stimulate discussion and serve as a source of ideas and inspiration to the profession.

PART ONE: FOUR-YEAR COLLEGES

1 | *SUMMARY OF FINDINGS*

Questionnaires were sent to 2,176 four-year departments on the MLA mailing list. Of those departments, 693 (31.8%) returned the form; an additional 18 (.8%) responded by letter and/or other descriptive materials such as catalogues, brochures, program evaluations, and annual reports; 29 departments (1.3%) sent letters or notes explaining that their particular situation was so dismal that they saw no utility in providing figures; 36 (1.6%) reported that they did not teach or were no longer teaching foreign languages; and 8 departments (.4%), protesting the detailed information requested by the questionnaire and the insufficient time for answering, returned it uncompleted. Subtracting those departments that did not offer any foreign language instruction, the total questionnaire response rate amounted to 33.2%. It must be pointed out, however, that many departments did not submit the complete data requested. Surprisingly, a number of chairpersons claimed they did not have easy access to departmental or institutional enrollment figures.

Because the response rate on the questionnaires was relatively low and because no efforts were made to randomize or stratify sampling procedures, the numerical data presented here should not be considered accurate in the statistical sense or representative of the total curricular picture in the United States. Judging from many written comments, it is probably realistic to assume that the sample described is a biased one and that a large number of institutions did not respond because they considered their curriculum "unsuccessful" in terms of generating student interest and felt that they could contribute little to the stated purpose of the study.

With few exceptions, foreign language enrollments fell during the period investigated. Only 157 departments (23%) reported enrollment growth proportionate to total institutional growth. The responding sample reported a total loss of 26,312 students (9.1%). German showed the largest loss (18.5%), followed by French (16.2%), Russian (10.8%), Latin (6%), and Italian (2.3%). Only Spanish reported an overall increase in enrollments (2.5%).

Accompanying the drop in general undergraduate enrollments was a decline in the number of majors and teaching staff. The responding departments indicated a total decrease of 802 majors (10.1%) between 1972 and 1976. French reported a 19.4% decline in majors, German 12.1%, Latin 9.5%, and even Spanish (the only commonly taught language that showed an overall enrollment increase) showed a 3.2% decrease in majors. Only Russian and Italian indicated small gains in majors. Finally, the total loss in teaching staff amounted to 437 full-time positions (7.4%) and 50 teaching assistantships (2.4%).

For an analysis of the responding sample and complete statistics on overall foreign language enrollments, majors, and faculty positions, see Appendix B.

The responses to those questions dealing with foreign language requirements present a complex picture and are difficult to quantify. Requirement patterns are so complicated and diverse that occasionally even chairpersons do not appear to know or understand them fully; in several cases, different department heads from the same institution gave conflicting information pertaining to requirements.

Of the 541 institutions that responded by questionnaire, a total of 300 (55%) reported a loss of, or a reduction in, foreign language requirements since 1968: 136 (25%) had abolished a general degree requirement since 1968 (98, or 18%, had done so between 1968 and 1972, while 38, or 7%, followed suit after 1972); and 164 colleges (30%) had reduced requirements since 1968 (67 or 12%, between 1968 and 1972 and 87, or 16%, since 1972).

Reductions of requirements took many forms. Some institutions decreased the number of required courses or credits. Others instituted either/or options (e.g., mathematics or foreign language) or changed to a distribution requirement in which students choose among courses from several disciplines, including foreign languages. Some institutions began to liberalize placement procedures or to exempt students with a specified number of years of high school foreign language study. Still others have added new programs or degrees not requiring a foreign language, and some disciplines or degrees that required a foreign language in the past no longer do so.

On the positive side, 19 responding institutions (3.5%) have introduced, reinstituted, or increased foreign language requirements since 1968 (4 in fall 1977), and 16 (3%) plan active discussion of reinstatement or an increase of requirements in the near future.

For those institutions that require some form of foreign language study, the ways in which requirements can be fulfilled vary considerably. Of the respondents, 84 institutions (15%) list entrance requirements, usually two years of high school study, but occasionally one or three. (Generally, however, entrance requirements are not strictly enforced; often a student can make up or complete the requirement after enrolling in college.) While 89 colleges (16%) list some form of foreign language requirement for all students enrolled, regardless of degree, 109 (20%) require foreign language study only for the B.A. degree. Departmental or divisional requirements, rather than general degree requirements, are listed by 147 institutions (27%). Finally, in 42 institutions (8%), foreign languages are an option of general education, distribution, or humanities requirements. The number of credit hours required by various institutions, departments, or degrees also varies widely, ranging from 2 to 24. (One institution requires intermediate proficiency in *two* languages.) The average requirement, however, is 12 semester hours, or intermediate proficiency.

Those institutions with some form of foreign language requirement list a range of options in addition to conventional introductory and intermediate language skills courses to fulfill the requirement. Of the 693 respondents, 364 departments (52.5%) permit credit by placement or proficiency exam, while 78 (11.2%) accept courses in more than one foreign language (e.g., two semesters of introductory French plus two semesters of introductory German). Special tracks in reading, conversation, translation, and so forth are offered by 70 departments (10.1%). While 60 departments (8.6%) permit fulfillment of requirement by culture/civilization or linguistics courses taught in English, 54 (7.8%) accept literature in translation courses. Many institutions automatically waive the requirement for students with a set number of years of high school foreign language study, some give automatic college credit for introductory language courses to those freshmen able to complete an intermediate course with a specified grade.

It is interesting to note that the following disciplines still consider foreign language study helpful or essential to their majors (disciplines are listed in the order of frequency with which they appeared on the questionnaires): English, music, history, chemistry, biology, religious studies, art, mathematics, political science, physics, art history, education, psychology, drama, social sciences, philosophy, anthropology, radio/TV broadcasting, geology, economics, journalism, and sociology.

The 693 four-year departments responding to the questionnaire reported almost 1,800 new courses developed and offered between 1972 and 1976. Most of these courses fell into the traditional domain of foreign language and literature study. For instance, many institutions reported introductory and intermediate instruction in languages not previously taught; introductory and intermediate conversation tracks and courses proliferated, as did culture/civilization courses and courses dealing with literary masterpieces, genres, authors, periods, or general literary surveys for advanced students or foreign language majors.

What follows is a selected list of course titles, grouped under general headings indicating major areas of course development (excluding traditional skills and literature courses). An asterisk indicates that similar courses have been developed in languages other than that specified in the title.

Culture/Civilization/History
  *Soviet Man and His World
  *USSR: Country and People
  Introduction to French Life and Civilization
  *Introduction to French Thought
  *The French Press
  *The French Heritage in America
  *Topical Readings in French Culture
  Traveling through France
  Christmas in Paris

Aller et Retour
Francophone Civilizations outside France
Voices of the French Speaking World
*Contemporary French Living
France: May 1968
*The Making of Contemporary France
L'Histoire de Paris
Les Monuments de Paris
Paris—Cultural Center of France
Black Expression in French
French Images of America
From Cubism to Surrealism
Le Château, centre de la culture et de la littérature
*German Culture through Literature
*Panorama of German Culture
*German Civilization as Reflected in Music
*Readings in German Culture and Thought
Literature and Culture of the Weimar Years
Germany and World War II
Decadent Germany
Political Profiles of the Two Germanies
Germany: East and West
The Other Germany
Impact of German Immigration on America
Those Strange German Ways
The German Crises
German Contributions to Western Civilization
Berlin in the Twentieth Century
Berlin, 1918–1933
*Issues and Problems in German Society
Vienna
The Viennese *Volkstheater*
The Austrian Experience
*Scandinavian Heritage
*Scandinavian Immigrant Culture
*Spanish Civilization as Reflected in the Arts
*Life Styles in Latin America
Missions in Mexico
The Chicano Experience
Chicano Expressive Culture
The Bullfight
Hispanic Minorities in the United States
The Culture of Latino Groups in the United States
Intercultural Studies: Latin America
Reform and Revolution in Latin America
Italian Opera
The Italian/American Experience
The Individual in Athens and Rome
The Private Life of Ancient Romans
Mythology and History
*Archeology
*The Art of Ancient Israel
Religion and Culture of Ancient India
Japanese Tea Ceremony

*Semiotics
Foreign Influences on American Culture

Special Themes Courses
    Insanity in Literature
    The Writer and Society
    The Writer as a Critic of Society
    Literature and Politics
    The Hero in Literature
    Introspection and Revolt
    Utopia in Literature
    Literature and the Drug Experience
    Fate and Free Will in Heroic Literature
    Women in Antiquity
    *Intellectual Background of Twentieth-Century French Literature
    Christian Perspectives in French Literature
    America in French Literature
    French Feminine Fiction
    Visions de la femme
    Existential Women
    Négritude
    Germany: The Search for Honor and Glory
    *Women in German Culture
    *Images of Women in German Literature
    Women: Center of Cultural, Social, and Political Endeavors in the Middle Ages
    Love, War, and the Other World in Medieval German Literature
    Social Protest in German Drama
    Mysticism in Indian Literature
    Common Themes in English and Asian Literature
    Taoism, Creativity, and Literature
    Women in Asia
    Third World Women
    The Age of Crisis in Modern Hebrew Literature
    Holocaust and Resistance
    *Perspectives of Man in Italian Literature
    Freedom in Russian Literature
    Justice in Russian Literature
    Revolution in Soviet Literature
    Satire in Russian Theater
    Soviet Dissidents
    *Social Themes in Latin American Literature
    Feminine Authors in Hispanic Literature
    *The Woman in Scandinavian Literature

Career-Related and Special Skills Courses
    *French for Travelers
    French for the World of Work
    *Scientific French
    German Vocal Music
    *German Phonetics for Music and Broadcasting Majors
    *Technical German
    Italian through Opera
    *Italian for Tourists
    Italian Conversation for Medicine and Business

Commercial Polish
*Russian for Singers
*Russian for Science Students
Russian Scientific Thought
*Russian for Reading and Research
*Business Russian
Spanish for Medical Personnel
Spanish for Community Workers
Spanish for Law Enforcement Personnel
Spanish for the Service Professions
Spanish for Health Personnel
*Spanish for Hotel Management Personnel
Spanish for Airline Personnel
Spanish for Teachers
Spanish for Preprofessionals
Spanish for Mining Personnel
Spanish for Urban Workers
Career Spanish
Public Service Spanish
Technical Translation

Conversation Courses
Liberated Expression in French
*Survival French
*Practicum in German
*Essential Japanese
*Everyday Spanish
*Functional Spanish
*Practical Spanish
*Oral Russian
*Intensive Oral Practice in Russian

Vocabulary Building
The Roots of Scientific and Legal Terminology
Foreign Elements in Hebrew
Latin and Greek Elements in English
Latin Etymology
Vocabulary Building through Foreign Language Study

Reading
*Reading Knowledge in Spanish
*Reading in Russian Periodicals
*Readings in the French Press

Special
Spanish for Native and Near-Native Speakers
Computer Application in Language and Literature
Migrant Internship

General Introduction to Language/Culture
    The Individual, Culture, and the World
    Ethnic Roots and Intercultural Themes
    The Search for Values in Humanistic Disciplines
    Cross-Cultural Expression
    Images of Man
    Concepts of Language
    Communication and Culture
    Intercultural Experiences
    Studies in Foreign Cultures
    The Nature of Language
    Language and Man

Techniques of Translation/Interpretation
    *Problems of Literary Translation
    *Practicum in Translation
    *Technical Translation
    *Techniques in Simultaneous Intepretation
    Techniques in Consecutive Interpretation

Thematic Film Courses
    Film and German Mentality
    The Japanese Film as Literature
    *Film as a Reflection of French Culture

Folklore
    Folktales in Africa
    Oral Narrative in Africa
    Chinese Folk Religion
    German Childrens' Literature
    Introduction to World Folk Literature
    Nordic Sagas
    Northern Mythology
    *Fairy Tales
    *The Oral Arts

Courses Implying Non-Traditional Teaching Approaches
    *Intensive German
    *Accelerated Spanish
    *Individualized Spanish
    *Decelerated French
    French through the Total Physical Response Method
    *Self-Paced French
    French by Television

In addition to the programs listed above, many courses were listed repeat-edly by several institutions. Literature in translation and history of the language courses were reported for all languages taught. There were also a number of linguistics courses, including phonetics, contrastive analysis, and applied linguistics; two Spanish departments offered courses in sociolinguistics. Classical mythology courses, taught in translation, were highly successful in attracting students. Finally, in addition to the thematic film courses listed above, there were film courses in French, German, Indian, Italian, Japanese, and Spanish and courses in play production in Spanish, French, and German.

Following is a summary of responses indicating the number of departments offering innovative or non-traditional courses and/or methodological approaches.

Type of course/approach	Number of departments indicating availability[a]	
Literature in translation	443	(64%)
Intensive or accelerated courses	346	(50%)
Contemporary culture (taught in FL)	331	(48%)
Introduction to language/linguistics	327	(47%)
Programs abroad (total)	316	(46%)
Programs abroad (summer)	123	(18%)
Programs abroad (academic year)	193	(28%)
Interdisciplinary courses (total)	308	(44%)
staffed within one department	113	(16%)
staffed by two or more departments	195	(28%)
Special topics courses, major focus on language and literature	263	(38%)
Career-related courses	218	(31%)
Contemporary culture (taught in English)	166	(24%)
Community-oriented courses aimed at special non-matriculating students	159	(23%)
Comparative literature	150	(22%)
Team teaching	145	(21%)
Area studies (taught in English)	124	(18%)
Internships	118	(17%)
Special themes, major focus not on language or literature	111	(16%)
Translation of specialized materials	98	(14%)
Area studies (taught in FL)	97	(14%)
Language courses for native speakers	76	(11%)
Off-campus courses	55	(8%)
Comparative cultures (taught in English)	50	(7%)
Ethnic studies (taught in FL)	47	(7%)
Comparative cultures (taught in FL)	45	(6%)
Ethnic studies (taught in English)	42	(6%)
Multilanguage or exploratory courses	40	(6%)
Courses in which use of media is a major integrated component:		
Audio/tape (including language lab)	253	(36%)
Film	165	(24%)
Slide/filmstrip	164	(24%)
Multimedia	86	(12%)
Television	46	(7%)
Computer-assisted instruction	26	(4%)
Radio	7	(1%)
Individualized instruction		
One-to-one tutorial or small group instruction	154	(22%)
Self-paced instruction	74	(11%)
Audio-tutorial, independent study	72	(10%)
Minicourses geared to special student interest	43	(6%)
Programmed instruction	40	(6%)

[a] Percentages rounded to nearest whole number

Departments offering less commonly taught languages

Chinese	32	(5%)
Japanese	27	(4%)
Hebrew	24	(3%)
Portuguese	23	(3%)
Greek	25	(3%)
Arabic	20	(3%)
Serbo-Croatian	12	(2%)
Italian	12	(2%)
Russian	11	(2%)
Swahili	10	(1%)
Czech	8	(1%)
Swedish	8	(1%)
Korean	7	(1%)
Polish	7	(1%)
Dutch	7	(1%)
Norwegian	7	(1%)
Persian	6	(less than 1%)
Hindi	6	"
Thai	5	"
Sanskrit	5	"
Bulgarian	5	"
Indonesian	5	"
Romanian	5	"
Turkish	4	"
Tagalog	4	"
Yiddish	4	"
Danish	4	"

Sixty other languages (mostly African, Asian and American Indian) were offered by one or two departments.

Of the 693 responding departments, 437 (63%) use some type of test for placement purposes: 218 departments (31%) have developed their own examinations; the remaining 219 (32%) use scores on a standardized test for placement purposes. The most frequently listed placement instruments were the MLA Cooperative Tests (126 departments, or 18%), College Entrance Examination Board-CEEB (44 departments, or 6%), College Level Examination Programs-CLEP (13 departments, or 2%), and the Pimsleur Achievement Test (11 departments, or 2%).

Only 7 departments (1%) reported regular systematic administration of an aptitude test to beginning foreign language students. The Carroll-Sapon Modern Language Aptitude Test (MLAT) and the Pimsleur Language Aptitude Battery (LAB) were the tests most frequently mentioned for this purpose.

Six departments (less than 1%) reported the use of some form of attitude measurement. All such tests, which appear to be constructed locally, measure attitudes toward foreign cultures and foreign language learning. A number of departments indicated that some attitudinal questions are part of a final course evaluation.

Regular, systematic, departmental achievement/proficiency testing was indicated by only 190 departments (27%). While 100 departments (14%) devise their own tests, 90 (13%) listed standardized tests such as the MLA Cooperative Tests, CEEB, the Graduate Record Exam (GRE), the College Board Achievement Test, and examinations developed by the professional organizations for the various languages.

2 | MAJOR PROBLEMS

The most commonly listed reasons for the decline in foreign language enrollments in four-year institutions fall into six categories: 1) changing requirements; 2) change in student attitudes and abilities; 3) budget constraints; 4) quality of advising and negative attitudes among non-foreign language faculty; 5) reduced quality and quantity of high school programs; and 6) diversification and proliferation of new majors and of less commonly taught languages.

Most responding departments agree that one of the major reasons for enrollment losses is the elimination or reduction of degree requirements. There are only a few exceptions to this consensus: Several departments of less commonly taught languages and some Latin and Slavic departments reported that reduction or elimination of the requirement has had a positive effect on enrollments in their respective languages. Of the 541 responding institutions, 300 (55%) have had a change in degree requirements during the past eight years in the form of either total abolishment, a reduction in the number of courses required, or a change from a pure foreign language requirement to one in which a foreign language is an option among several offerings.

A few departments claim that, while they initially lost some enrollments, they have actually benefited from the elimination of requirements in terms of higher quality students, heightened achievement among students, more positive attitudes among students *and* instructors, more enjoyable working conditions, and improved instructional quality from teachers who realize that special efforts must be made to hold "volunteers." In the words of one chairperson, "without the prop of an externally imposed curricular subsidy, our teaching must be imaginative and sophisticated, and all our students are in our language courses because they wish to be."

The second most frequently mentioned cause of decline in foreign language enrollments was a perceived change in student attitudes and abilities. Many respondents listed an increased pragmatism and career orientation on the part of students. The greatly reduced job market for foreign language teachers and limited employment possibilities for graduates with B.A. degrees in foreign languages have discouraged many talented students from specializing in foreign languages. Respondents also noted decreased student interest in a liberal arts curriculum and humanistic studies on the one hand and a seemingly contradictory increase in the popularity of non-specialist degrees such as "general studies majors" on the other. Since many general studies programs are individually designed and most "generalist" students seem to avoid the rigors of foreign language study, even the latter trend usually affects foreign language study adversely. (Again there is an exception to the rule: The University of Michigan reports an increase of enrollments because of general studies majors.)

Some chairpersons believe that because of lower admissions standards at many institutions, students enter college with less formal training in languages (and especially less preparation in English) and are generally less able than in previous years to undertake systematic foreign language study. Further, fewer students appear willing to make the necessary commitment of time and energy and to submit themselves to the mental discipline that language study requires. One respondent summarized the situation by stating that students gravitate toward those courses or programs that appear easy and enhance their employment opportunities.

The third most frequently listed reason for enrollment losses was the vicious circle syndrome of budget cuts → faculty reduction (often stripping a department of all non-tenured faculty and much flexibility) → reduction in courses → loss of students → more budget reductions, and so on. Again, it should be noted that several departments have been able to rally to the cause by redistributing assignments or accepting overloads, thereby actually increasing enrollments despite loss of faculty.

Another frequently mentioned cause of waning enrollments was a lack of communication between departments, often reflected in the indifferent quality of advising or in negative attitudes and lack of support by advisers, colleagues in other fields, and administrators. Certainly, the influence of an adviser in guiding students to, and away from, certain courses and disciplines should not be underestimated.

Many respondents attributed declining enrollments in part to the reduced quality and quantity of high school foreign language programs. There are conflicting opinions as to whether high school foreign language study benefits or hurts enrollments on the college level. Some chairpersons claim that a number of students place beyond a requirement or earn credit by examination because of improved high school instruction, thereby reducing enrollments in introductory college courses. Some maintain that high school foreign language instruction engenders negative student attitudes and often discourages continuation of study on the college level. Russian and classics departments seem relatively unified in believing that the almost total loss of a high school base in those languages has had a negative effect on enrollments in upper-level college courses. On the other hand, the erosion of foreign language study on the high school level generally has contributed to increased enrollments in lower-division college courses, especially in those institutions that still have a language requirement. The major problem appears to be one of articulation, communication, and cooperation among the various instructional levels.

A number of respondents indicated that diversification of options has also contributed to enrollment declines. The introduction of less commonly taught languages or languages appealing to particular ethnic groups has detracted from enrollments in the more popular languages. But again, there is no unanimous agreement concerning the effect of adding languages to the curricular offerings. A few departments indicated that diversification of linguistic offerings has contributed to overall departmental growth and that, generally, students who opt for a less commonly taught language have rather special motivations and interests. Some educators believe that the proliferation of new majors (e.g., ethnic studies, urban studies, area studies, communications) and the open competition for majors by other departments have affected the language requirement and the number of majors in foreign languages. Several complained that many professional programs are overstructured and leave little room for electives, particularly for a sequence of courses necessary to gain some proficiency in a foreign language.

In examining the causes given for declining enrollments, it becomes obvious that most of us look for the culprit(s) outside our own departmental domain. While many chairpersons listed improved instructional quality and increased enthusiasm and commitment on the part of the faculty as major reasons for enrollment increases, only one blamed enrollment decline on low quality of instruction and apathy of teaching staff. Yet it would appear obvious that, if quality of instruction can have a positive effect, it can also affect student interest negatively.

Roger Peel of Middlebury College is one of the foreign language educators who believe that causes for enrollment losses are to be found largely *within* the ranks of the profession. He blames traditionalism and a collective lack of imagination for the present state of affairs. Generally speaking, one might tend to agree with him when looking at college catalogues from institutions that have for decades offered basically the same courses, the same uninspiring course descriptions, and the same traditional divisions into introductory and intermediate language followed by third- and fourth-year literature courses.

3 | *FACTORS INFLUENCING ENROLLMENT GROWTH*

The factors credited with contributing to enrollment growth at four-year institutions differ from department to department, even from language to language. There seems to be no simple answer to increasing interest in foreign language study. *There is no single approach (or even combination of approaches) that a department can adopt in order to guarantee success in increasing either achievement or enrollment.*

Often, program growth is attributable largely to external factors that are not under the direct control of an institution or department. Obviously, total institutional growth contributes (or at least should contribute) to rising departmental enrollments. Demographic factors and a renewed ethnic awareness contribute to the increased popularity of Spanish in parts of the Southwest, West, and East where there are large settlements of people of Hispanic origin, and to the popularity of other languages in population centers with large Italian, Japanese, Chinese, or French components. Conversely, ethnic awareness is not as pronounced among people of northern European extraction; one reason for the decrease in the popularity of German, for instance, might be the assimilation of peoples of Germanic origins into the dominant culture of the United States. Ironically, while large ethnic concentrations often increase undergraduate enrollments, they sometimes decrease graduate enrollments. For example, a knowledge of Spanish can bring immediate employment opportunities in some parts of the country. A case in point is the University of California, where the easy employability of recent recipients of the B.A. in Spanish is believed to be a factor contributing to declining interest in graduate programs.

External factors alone are no guarantee of program success in terms of enrollment increases. To a large extent it is still up to departmental initiative and imagination to appeal to the "ready-made markets" of students by developing attractive and relevant options to accommodate various interests. This point is illustrated by a number of institutions located in heavily Spanishpopulated areas that have actually suffered decreases in enrollments and by the many institutions that have experienced departmental losses despite institutional enrollment increases.

The most commonly mentioned "internal" reasons for enrollment gains (or increase in student interest) can be grouped into several major categories: quality of instruction; departmental diversification in terms of non-traditional options courses; intensive courses; study abroad; course credit options; special methodological approaches; out-of-classroom activities; and recruiting, publicizing, and advising.

Instructional Quality

A large number of chairpersons acknowledged increased teaching effectiveness by an energetic, enthusiastic, imaginative, and accessible faculty as a major factor in attracting students. The influence of instructional quality on a program cannot be too strongly emphasized: In the final analysis, it is the individual teacher's commitment and creativity that determine program success. In a number of departments, single individuals—teachers and administrators—were credited as being *the* cause for attracting increasing numbers of students.

Based on the findings of this study, enrollment increases, where there have been any, have been predominantly in lower-division courses. Apart from those few institutions that serve uniquely or predominantly as graduate training centers, lower-division language instruction is the financial lifeblood of all departments, and what goes on in introductory courses determines to a large extent student interest and motivation for continued language study. In other words, the lower-division courses are the recruiting centers for intermediate and advanced language study. Not all departments appear to recognize the importance of coordination and articulation of introductory language programs. Lower-division courses are occasionally used as "load fillers"—i.e., they are assigned to teaching staff to provide a full teaching load without regard to individual interests or suitability to teach these courses. Instruction often appears haphazard, with few efforts at coordinating and articulating objectives and instructional outcomes at each level. Objectives are most often expressed only in the number of chapters to be covered. Otherwise, there seems to be no common planning, no common focus, no common evaluation, despite multiple sections and a number of individuals teaching the course.

Some institutions list as a major factor for their success the utilization of senior faculty on all levels of instruction, not just in advanced language and literature courses. Excellent instruction, positive student reaction, and impressive language proficiency have also been observed in programs utilizing teaching assistants in lower-division language courses. Invariably, at such institutions considerable time and effort are devoted to the coordination of multisection courses and to the training, guidance, and supervision of teaching assistants. The University of Michigan, the University of California at Berkeley, and the University of Southern California are examples of institutions where much attention is given to the daily coordination of introductory language programs.

Obligatory evaluations (by students, colleagues, and department administrators), which are being used in decisions regarding salary increases, promotions, reappointment, or tenure, were also mentioned by several departments as having had some influence on improving quality of instruction.

Non-Traditional Options Courses

Program diversification has been a key element in the growth of most departments visited. Institutions report a proliferation of literature in translation courses, culture courses taught in English, or other options to the traditional literary offerings. Some departments indicate that these newly developed options not only have enabled them to survive in recent crisis years but occasionally have stimulated interest in traditional language skills courses as well.

Clearly, literature in translation courses have been the most popular curricular addition. Of the 693 responding four-year departments, 443 (64%) offer such courses. Next in popularity among options courses are introduction to language/linguistics courses, which are listed by 327 (47%) departments. In addition, 166 (24%) departments offer contemporary culture courses taught in English; 150 (22%) offer comparative literature courses; and 40 (6%) offer multilanguage or exploratory language courses.

It appears that diversification has especially benefited Slavic, classics, German, and Italian departments. Since these languages pose greater difficulty for English speakers, their literatures are less accessible in their original forms than are French and Spanish literatures. Moreover, although few students formally study languages except for French and Spanish on the secondary and college levels, many have an interest in other cultures and civilizations.

With the obvious exception of offerings in classics (where mythology and terminology courses are popular options), among the especially successful courses are those that focus on current cultural aspects and modern authors or works (particularly those courses that relate literature to social, historical, or philosophical themes in present-day life). Some examples of such courses are: "Insanity in Literature" (College of St. Scholastica); "Literature and the Drug Experience" (Washington State University); "The Search for Honor and Glory" (Franklin and Marshall College); "Freedom in Russian Literature" (Loyola University, New Orleans); "Women in French Literature" (several institutions); "Literature and Politics" (Tufts University, German); "Insiders and Outsiders: Literature and Culture of the Weimar Years" (Middlebury College); "Decadent Germany" (Jacksonville State University); and "Impact of German Immigration on America" (Elmhurst College). (For additional course titles, see chapter i.)

Film courses taught predominantly in English are another popular nontraditional option. They draw numbers of students not usually interested in traditional language courses, and they can be offered on all levels of instruction. Film courses are used for a range of purposes and student interests. The emphasis can be on language study, cinematographic techniques, analysis of artistic composition, cultural analysis, or comparative culture study focusing on specific themes.

Several institutions have begun to accept non-traditional courses to fulfill a language requirement or have developed special options courses for that purpose. As can be expected, feelings are ambivalent among faculty in departments that have chosen to accept so-called options and translation courses to fulfill a general language requirement. Many colleagues admit that the move was motivated by the department's struggle for survival when having to compete with requirement options in mathematics, computer language, or general humanities offerings. A growing number of foreign language educators are convinced, however, that the traditional language skills course and the expectation of mastery of a foreign language are not valid as general requirements.

External factors have contributed to increased offerings in two additional non-traditional options: interdisciplinary majors and career-related courses. While job opportunities for academically oriented foreign language specialists appear to be decreasing, at least in the commonly taught languages, the need for professionals with some insights in, and knowledge of, foreign languages and cultures in practically all fields seems to be growing.

Some institutions actively encourage "interdisciplinary concentrations," "double majors," or "extended majors" in pamphlets and through departmental career conferences and counseling. A number of departments claim that interdisciplinary majors and/or courses have increased departmental enrollments. Of 308 departments, 44% list interdisciplinary offerings (113 [16%] with intradepartmental and 195 [28%] with interdepartmental staffing).

None of the schools visited, however, indicated full satisfaction with their involvement in interdisciplinary ventures. Upon closer inspection, many of the programs prove to be a mixture of courses in different departments, with the assumption that students will be able to synthesize on their own whatever interdisciplinary insights the sequence presents. This practice appears to dominate in area studies programs, for example. Often, a major obstacle to developing team-taught, interdisciplinary courses boils down to the difficulty of establishing an appropriate and fair division of FTE's among cooperating departments and thus rewarding individual faculty members for their efforts. Some departments attempt to utilize guest lectures to incorporate an interdisciplinary dimension. While this practice can be effective for an occasional course, on a regular basis the guest speakers would perhaps find the commitment too time-consuming. Well-coordinated interdisciplinary courses demand much time for joint planning, preparation, and coordination. Ideally, all members of the teaching team should attend each lecture to offer true interdisciplinary reaction, interaction, and synthesis. Truly interdisciplinary programs relating knowledge of a foreign language and culture and introducing a comparative culture dimension into the social sciences, arts, humanities, and professional schools should be developed. Such programs, by necessity, must be interdepartmental, team-taught efforts, since few instructors are equally competent in several fields.[7]

The need for language skills in various professions has also contributed to an increase in career-related courses. While two-year institutions have generally been more active in providing specialized career-supportive foreign language courses, several four-year departments are also making efforts to develop such programs. These offerings usually attract a relatively small number of students, but they appear to have a favorable effect on departmental visibility in the community, engendering positive reaction among students, faculty of cooperating departments, and community agencies that provide internships, field experiences, and jobs for the students involved.

Spanish leads in developing career-related foreign language instruction because of practical necessity in areas with large Spanish-speaking populations. Conversational Spanish courses aimed at secretaries, law enforcement personnel, prospective clergymen, the medical professions, and workers in social service agencies and the tourist industry are proliferating. (Weber State College, for instance, reports much interest in its career-oriented conversational Spanish courses for law enforcement officers, nurses, and medical and paramedical officers.) Occasionally, institutions take instruction off campus at the request of various community agencies, such as police and fire departments or hospitals. Both San Antonio College and the Rose-Hulman Institute of Technology offer a two-year program in technical translation, which in the case of the latter institution has been mentioned as an important factor in generating student interest.

Although Spanish leads in the number of career-related courses, other languages have developed similar programs. The German Department of the University of Cincinnati has developed an undergraduate international business option,[8] while some institutions offer special courses in diction for music and communications majors, or special etymology and technical terminology courses for the medical and legal professions, for art historians, and for majors in political sciences. (For other titles of career-supportive courses, see chapter i.)

Related to the need for emphasizing pragmatic, career-related objectives in foreign language instruction, several institutions are offering certificates of proficiency. At Illinois Wesleyan University this certificate becomes a part of the student's career placement file, indicating to prospective employers and/or graduate schools that the student possesses superior linguistic and cultural skills in addition to training in the major field.[9] Rutgers University (Slavics) also offers a certificate of proficiency. Rather than using an internally developed proficiency examination, the University of Arkansas at Fayetteville is experimenting with the *Zertifikat Deutsch als Fremdsprache,* developed jointly by the Goethe Institute and the *Deutscher Volkschochschulverband* and recognized as an indicator of basic proficiency in German by all Common Market countries.

With few exceptions (e.g., the University of Cincinnati and the University of South Carolina), the career-supportive courses are taught at the lower-division level. Although these offerings are certainly valid services to the student body and the community, language proficiency gained in one or two semesters of specially developed career-oriented courses is necessarily limited and often consists only of an emergency vocabulary for a small number of situations. Career-related foreign language instruction should be extended to the advanced and graduate levels. *After* acquiring a general foundation in a foreign language, students should have options other than traditional literature courses to further their language proficiency.

Intensive Courses

In many institutions where intensive courses are a regular option in the curriculum, such courses also rate high among the factors that leave students with positive attitudes toward language study and contribute to initial enrollment and retention of students in upper-level courses. Of the 693 responding four-year institutions, 346 (50%) list some form of intensive offering; among the 182 responding two-year institutions, only 23 (13%) list the availability of intensive instruction.

Intensive programs have no common definition. They range from the total immersion program at the Middlebury Summer School, complete with a language pledge (i.e., a signed promise to use only the target language as means of communication for the duration of the course), to an intensive Saturday course (meeting every Saturday for six hours of instruction) offered by the Department of French and Italian Languages and Literatures at the University of Maryland at College Park. In between come intensive summer programs offering from two to four semesters' credit (e.g., Washington State University), intensive semesters (North Texas State University), and intensive year-round programs (Dartmouth and Pomona College).

Any course meeting more than the traditional fifty-minute period per day can carry the label intensive. In some institutions the only difference between a regular course and an intensive course is that the latter meets two instructional periods rather than one per day, but staff, objectives, materials, and teaching strategies remain constant. Some departments, while not actually listing intensive instruction in the catalogue, make an intensive exposure of up to seven hours a week available by scheduling courses that may be taken simultaneously by students. For instance, in addition to the conventional three- or four-hour course, students can enroll in a one- to three-hour conversation course, reading course, pronunciation clinic, group drill session, and/or laboratory period.

Another form of intensive exposure is provided by special residential language houses such as those at Pomona College, Middlebury College, and the University of Michigan. While in residence, for credit or non-credit, students have systematic opportunities to engage in formal or informal conversation with fluent speakers of the target language and can (or are expected to) use the target language constantly. They participate in additional lectures, films, or other programs dealing with the target language or culture and can obtain tutorial help from residents fluent in the language.

It appears, however, that those programs utilizing differentiated staffing (i.e., more than one instructor, each with special competencies and functions), differentiated activities (i.e., separately scheduled activities, such as grammar explication sessions, drill sessions, culture presentations, use of games, songs, interaction or conversation sessions, and alternating small-group work with large-group instruction), a direct methodology, and a variety of materials and media are considered particularly attractive and effective by students. Moreover, such programs appear to retain more students for future foreign language study than those courses that simply condense the time element and do not otherwise differentiate instruction.

The advantages of intensive programs over conventional ones are easily summarized: 1) they expose students to a concentrated body of language and facilitate more intensive and extensive skill practice, therefore resembling, more than their traditional one-hour-per-day counterparts, a natural language learning situation; 2) they enable students to gain extensive knowledge of, and proficiency in, the language without the usual lengthy time commitments; 3) they permit "late bloomers," procrastinating seniors, and Ph.D. candidates to fulfill a language requirement or a long-standing interest or ambition, again in a relatively short amount of time and without penalty in terms of postponed graduation; 4) they permit students majoring in various disciplines to elect a supportive concentration in a foreign language; 5) they provide high school seniors, "professional tourists," and businessmen a quick, concentrated introduction or refresher course in a language; and 6) from highly positive reactions observed at some programs visited, they promote an easy camaraderie among students and faculty, and, as mentioned already, often motivate further language study.

It appears that the large majority of intensive courses, apart from special summer programs, are taught on the introductory/intermediate level. Exceptions, in which intensive instruction has been implemented on more advanced levels, are at Middlebury College and the University of Texas at Arlington, where an intensive German course is taught on the third-year level. More experimentation should be conducted with intensive instruction at advanced levels. Certainly, foreign language majors and other students with a basic background in a language could benefit from intensive exposure to, or extended immersion in, the language to "activate" their knowledge and improve their fluency.

Intensive instruction also poses problems. One is what to do with the student who, for some reason or other, cannot complete a program and loses up to an entire term of course credit because it is too late to enroll in or transfer to other courses. Some institutions are attempting to deal with this problem by enabling students to transfer freely to the next lower or concurrent conventionally taught course or by granting credit for coursework satisfactorily completed, even if a student does not finish the full intensive sequence. Another measure designed to prevent student failure is the insistence on individual counseling before permitting enrollment in intensive courses. It goes without saying that intensive foreign language study is not for everyone and that students need to be made aware of the motivation, commitment, energy, self-discipline, and plain hard work necessary in order to succeed.

Another potential drawback to intensive instruction mentioned by several instructors is that students engaging in short-term, intensive language instruction sometimes have difficulty retaining the subject matter. Intensive students, even though they cover the same syllabus as students in conventional instruction, may be at a disadvantage if they continue language study in traditional programs since they lack absorption or "digestion" time for the large quantity of materials presented. It would be interesting to conduct a follow-up study comparing rate of achievement and retention of subject matter among students from intensive and traditional programs.

Intensive courses require special efforts on the part of the teaching staff. Keeping students awake, alert, participating, and learning for several hours in succession is no small feat, even for a team of teachers. The needs for extensive planning, close cooperation and teamwork, and special creativity and enthusiasm should be carefully considered before embarking on an intensive instruction venture.

Study and Travel Abroad

As John B. Carroll points out, no other factor contributes as much to success in foreign language learning as does time spent in the target language country.[10] At those colleges that provide or actively encourage an integral study abroad experience (ranging from an interterm to a junior year abroad), student motivation and interest in lower- as well as in upper-level courses appear to be heightened. An impressive example is Dartmouth College, where a large percentage of the student body participate in programs abroad. Many students enrolled in introductory language courses mentioned an anticipated stay abroad as a major motivation for studying the target language. And a number of students majoring in various disciplines *other than* a foreign language serve as apprentice teachers (drill masters) in first-year language courses after returning from an experience abroad. Invariably, one of the reasons given for their continued interest in language study, despite demanding schedules in their major field of study, is that they have developed a deep interest in the target language and culture and want to maintain, practice, and improve their language skills. Also, for similar reasons, advanced courses in those institutions with active programs abroad attract a sizable number of non-majors.

Understandably, some departments that have to send their students to other schools for off-campus study are reluctant to encourage a stay abroad because they lose enrollments, and thus FTEs and income, while their students are affiliated with other institutions. But in the long run, the temporary loss of students might have positive effects by generating extended enthusiasm for advanced offerings.

Course Credit Options

In order to increase student interest in foreign language study, a number of institutions have modified traditional systems of awarding credits for foreign language courses. Two viable options are the reduction of credit/contact hours and variable course credit.

Several departments have adapted the credit and contact hours allotted to language courses to the general pattern prevailing at the institution. While language courses have traditionally required a larger number of contact hours than courses in other disciplines for the same number of credits (i.e., a four-credit language course often requires five contact hours plus additional lab or drill periods), some departments have gone to three-credit courses, requiring only three contact hours, without obligatory lab instruction. This pattern has the advantages of fitting the predominant Monday-Wednesday-Friday scheduling pattern at some institutions and of enabling more students to include a language course in their schedule. Such reduction of contact hours often requires an adjustment in course content as well, spreading the traditional first- or second-year content over three semesters. This reduction—or rather redistribution of course content—has been mentioned as a positive influence on student enrollments and has lessened attrition between levels at several institutions.

Another credit option is variable course credit. Often, students with some previous language instruction wish to maintain their skills but are not able to carry a full three- to five-hour course. One- to three-credit-hour courses focusing on a particular skill or topic appear to be quite popular for that purpose. Low-credit conversation or pronunciation courses, especially, draw an increasing number of students. Ohio State University grants variable course credit from one to ten credit hours for individualized basic language instruction in five languages. (See the description of Ohio State University's classics department in chapter iv.)

Special Methodological Approaches

Some departments attribute their success in attracting students to special psychologically or philosophically based methodologies or to particularly effective teaching techniques. The following instructional approaches are discussed below: the psycho-generative method, confluent education, direct methodology, individualized or self-paced instruction (including flexible testing and minicourses), the use of undergraduate assistants, media programs, and utilization of the language laboratory.

The University of Northern Iowa attributes its growth to the psycho-generative method developed and used there for instruction in introductory foreign language courses. This method utilizes a predominantly oral approach and teaches grammatical structures inductively based on five frames of reference: 1) the physical world (dealing with tangible things and places); 2) the frame of persons; 3) the frame of activities and actions; 4) the frame of events (time concepts, weddings, funerals, and so forth); and 5) the frame of perspective (dealing with personal judgments, opinions, and interpretations). The instructional materials developed for the approach use high-frequency vocabulary and grammatical structures. Students are taught to use a situational questioning method (the who, what, when, where, how, or why of each particular event). In addition to conventionally scheduled classroom instruction, students meet from two to four additional periods in small-group practice sessions, usually conducted by advanced undergraduate students. The psycho-generative method requires intensive and active student participation and appears to be successful with students who have shown low aptitude for foreign language learning with other methodologies.

Other successful programs are based on an instructional philosophy known as confluent education. Beverly Galyean reports significant changes in achievement and attitudes through confluent education techniques in an introductory French college course.[11] Borrowing from the values clarification and sensitivity training movements, confluent education stresses the *affective* development of the student. It recognizes the natural relationship between feelings and knowledge and emphasizes the development of interpersonal communication skills through special exercise techniques including Gestalt art works, guided fantasies, imagination games, non-verbal interaction strategies, improvisational theater, and values clarification exercises, all of which depend heavily on group processes.[12]

Galyean lists seven guidelines for designing a confluent model of instruction in foreign language teaching:

1) Students use their personal affective and cognitive content as the basis for meaningful language practice (as opposed to participating in rote-memory and impersonal practice).
2) Students talk directly to and with each other, exchanging information about real issues in their lives.
3) Students use the language for discovering information about themselves (introspection).
4) Students use the language for discovering information about the others (interpersonal relating).
5) Students direct their own learning activities by leading drills, exercises, and conversation groups.
6) Teachers relate to the students in a confluent-facilitative manner.
7) Teachers employ affective teaching methods.[13]

Confluent education techniques can be utilized in any setting. Like individualized instruction, confluent education is more a philosophy than a method.

While there is no existing single "confluent program," Hebrew Union College is experimenting with a confluent approach in introductory Hebrew instruction,[14] and several instructors in California adult education programs in French and Spanish report increased interest, motivation, and achievement because of confluent techniques. Galyean herself reports that one French instructor has tripled night enrollments since starting a confluent approach of instruction four years ago.[15]

The so-called confluent education movement is still predominantly based in California, but a number of foreign language educators mentioned that their programs had become more attractive because of greater stress on oral communication in the classroom and more personalized instructional techniques utilizing affective learning activities[16] and values clarification exercises.[17] Instead of practicing grammatical structures and vocabulary through mechanical patterns drills and repetition of personally meaningless dialogues between hypothetical persons from the target language culture, students engage in structured exercises to talk about their own concerns, feelings, and experiences.

A third methodological approach credited with contributing to positive student attitudes is direct teaching, which uses the target language as the exclusive medium of instruction and interaction. Apart from Middlebury College, where predominantly direct teaching has accomplished outstanding results in student fluency, the French Department at the University of California at Berkeley utilizes a "rationalist direct method," in which all new materials are first presented orally in the target language and a question/answer format is utilized to lead the students to inductive grammar generalizations. Students progress through a sequence of daily activities: performing → understanding → creating language, totally in French. At Portland Community College, there is a direct method program in German with highly impressive results in terms of student proficiency.

Another approach offers individualized instruction or self-paced programs. Such programs are no longer as widely available as the professional literature would make one believe, however. While many departments at one time or another experimented with some form of self-paced instruction, for a variety of reasons many have returned to a traditional "lock-step" pattern. Notable exceptions are the classics department at Ohio State University and the German and Italian programs at the University of California at Berkeley, where self-paced instruction is still thriving. But even Berkeley, which had an approximately equal distribution of students in the traditional and self-paced options, reports a decreasing interest in the individualized courses.

A major advantage of individualized instruction is, of course, that it permits students to move at their own learning speed. Advocates point out that self-pacing benefits especially the brighter and highly motivated students who can progress more quickly through the materials when they are not held back by the hypothetical "average learner" to whom instruction is geared in a conventional classroom. It is interesting to note, however, that students in individualized options tend to progress *more slowly* through the course, or end up with a *lower number of credit hours* earned per semester, than do students in conventional options. Unfortunately, no data have been collected that would permit comparison of student learning in traditional and self-paced courses after the lapse of a certain time period, to assess whether retention and mastery of subject matter are equally affected by both types of instruction.

While totally self-paced programs appear to have become less numerous, many departments have retained or incorporated components of individualized instruction that are regarded positively by students. For instance, while instruction at Tarrant County Junior College (Northeast Campus) is "lock-step," testing is on an individualized, self-paced basis, permitting students to retake differentiated forms of examinations as often as desired within the confines of the semester. These examinations are administered by the person in charge of the language laboratory and therefore do not make inordinate demands on instructor time.

Other institutions also permit flexible testing, and student reaction appears to be positive. Administrators at several institutions, however, expressed concern about "grade inflation." Undoubtedly, like instructors in other disciplines the survival of which depends on student enrollments, foreign language instructors have in the recent past collectively eased expectations somewhat and tended to show "mercy" in grading, hoping to retain students for further study. What, if anything, can or should be done about this practice, as long as administrations are impressed by numbers rather than by achievement, is not at issue in this discussion. To forestall any charges of "easy grading," however, departments considering flexible testing policies should insist that students earn their grades by actual mastery of content, regardless of how many tries it takes to achieve this mastery, rather than by memorization of test items from one test administration to the next (or, worse yet, by copying or other methods of cheating).

Minicourses are another means of "individualizing" content by providing options geared to particular student interests. The German Summer School at Middlebury College (see program description in chapter iv) offers a choice of minicourses (or modules) on the intermediate and third-year levels. These modules are offered not as independent self-instructional units but as a component of the traditional skills courses. Students can choose among a number of topics and projects of personal interest and work with small groups of similarly interested students.

While Winthrop College cannot claim an increase in student enrollment during the four-year period investigated, the department attributes its survival after the elimination of the language requirement to the offering of flexible minicourses. One-hour courses on the intermediate level such as "A Short Trip to French (or Spanish) Speaking Countries," "Readings in the French (or Spanish) Press," "Cross-Cultural Impressions," "French (Spanish or Mexican) Cooking," or modules focusing on selected French or Spanish readings have attracted much student interest. A flexible schedule permits students to enroll in several of these courses a semester, either as electives or in addition to the regular intermediate program.[18]

In addition to the programs discussed above, foreign language departments have tried a number of non-traditional instructional techniques. Several responding institutions utilize undergraduate students as instructional aides, drill masters, or apprentice teachers. Both Dartmouth and the University of Northern Iowa, for instance, have developed systems in which undergraduates with some fluency in a foreign language can participate actively in instruction of their peers. Dartmouth pays selected undergraduates to serve as daily "apprentice teachers" in small-group drill instruction. The oral drill sessions are strictly coordinated with the large-group periods taught by master teachers. Less threatened by their peers than by regular instructors, students react positively to peer instruction. Furthermore, seeing in the apprentice teacher a living example that it is possible to master the language undoubtedly has positive effects on their attitudes and willingness to invest large time blocks in language learning. The University of Northern Iowa uses undergraduate teaching assistants both as drill leaders during regular instructional periods and as tutors outside the classroom. Students are not paid for their services but can earn extra credit for assisting instructors in conducting small-group drill sessions. On a smaller scale, advanced undergraduate students give regular tutorial help in several institutions, either for pay or for "practicum" credit.

A number of departments also mentioned the use of media in language instruction as an effective means of attracting students. The University of Oregon has been very successful with the Spanish film series *Zarabanda* in introductory courses,[19] and Oregon State University has adapted both levels of the German *Guten Tag* series, making the filmed program available to the community for off-campus and continuing education credit in regular televised programs.[20] Media other than film have also been used to advantage by language departments. Luther College (Iowa) uses the computer for programmed exercises and testing. Generally speaking, many departments report using a large variety of media in instruction; completely mediated courses (i.e., courses totally based on computer-assisted instruction, videotape, film, tape, or media combinations without systematic group instruction) appear to be less attractive than one might expect, however, since once the newness wears off, many students become bored because of lack of group interaction. Programs with particularly well developed and integrated use of media in language instruction have been developed at Middlebury College and Tarrant County Junior College. Many of the materials used are locally developed and, unfortunately, are unavailable commercially.

Finally, several institutions mentioned effective utilization of the language laboratory as a factor that has contributed to increased student interest. Middlebury College, Pomona College, the University of Texas at El Paso, San Antonio College, and Tarrant County Junior College have made especially effective—and occasionally innovative—use of language laboratory facilities.

Anyone who has taught in an institution where the language lab was on its way to joining the dinosaurs will be especially interested in how the schools mentioned above not only have been able to retain the lab facilities as impressive monuments to technology but are using the facilities regularly to offer adjunct learning experiences to conventional instruction. Here are some points that language laboratory directors considered essential to effective utilization of the facilities:

1) All language labs that have been described as effective (in terms of learning) and successful (in terms of student use) are directed by a *full-time* person who, with the aid of work-study assistants, operates the facilities. Occasionally, these staff members offer a number of adjunct services to the department. For instance, they may manage the department's media materials, duplicate tapes for individual students and faculty, serve as tutors for students seeking individual help, manage the departmental resource library, administer tests, and so forth.

The appointment of a single director who considers managing the laboratory facilities as his or her primary function appears to be essential for effective utilization. Too often, attempts to staff the facilities solely with teaching assistants, work-study students, or faculty members who have major classroom teaching responsibilities are doomed to failure. While the person in charge of the laboratory does not necessarily need an extensive technical background or fluency in a foreign language (though it is obviously of great advantage if the director possesses knowledge and skills in both areas), he or she must have easy access to repair services either on or off campus. Some departments have been successful in funding a lab director position through library or learning resource center budgets. Others offer the laboratory facilities to English, music, and other departments on a cost-sharing basis.

2) Most colleges where the laboratory is actively used have moved (or are planning to move) from a central console to individual cassette units that permit greater variety of programming and greater flexibility in use. As in a library system, students can check out specific tapes they wish to work with and can progress at their own pace. Special cassettes permit recording of student responses while leaving the master program track unaltered.

3) For optimum effectiveness, the language lab should be open during regular times of instruction and also for periodic evening and weekend hours to accommodate working students.

4) While some of the departments with an obligatory attendance policy keep track of students with a time clock or with individual student sign-in cards, such systems of record keeping are cumbersome and time consuming and cause occasional resentment. In the opinion of the lab directors interviewed, the most effective and least resented system of enforcing language lab practice is the development of exercise sheets. These exercises are coordinated with each instructional unit, and students are required to submit completed sheets to their instructors at periodic time intervals. Work done in

the language lab counts as part of the final grade. The exercises devised for the language lab can consist of dictations, multiple-choice listening comprehension exercises, sound differentiation exercises, questions and answers on recorded passages, written summaries (in English) of recorded dialogues or narratives, written translations of spoken words or sentences, or any other type of exercise that lends itself to administration by tape recorded materials.

Using exercise sheets instead of a time clock to encourage laboratory use changes attendance from a time-oriented to a task-oriented requirement, one which is much less resented by students than an arbitrary number of hours or minutes imposed on all students regardless of their individual needs. Lab sheets do not require record keeping of student attendance since the completed sheet handed to the lab attendant or instructor is proof of attendance. The major problem of such a system, however, is that not all commercially available instructional series contain ready-made materials and instructors must therefore develop their own exercises and recordings. Obviously, the usual fare of taped pattern drills available with many older textbooks does not facilitate this kind of use.

5) Laboratory assignments must be coordinated with classroom instruction. If students see their work as unrelated or unrewarded (in terms of grades) in the course, motivation to use the lab becomes a problem. Exercises practiced in the language laboratory (e.g., dictations or listening comprehension exercises) can be systematically incorporated on classroom quizzes and examinations.

6) Language laboratory directors must keep up to date with new developments in lab facilities (the *NALLD Journal* is a good source of information) and suggest and encourage various uses to faculty members. Unfortunately, regardless of how up-to-date and well administered the facilities, the individual instructor still determines use of the laboratory by convincing the students of its value and by utilizing it where it can serve most effectively.

Out-of-Class Activities

The programs described in this section include regularly available curricular components (for credit or non-credit) that offer students an opportunity to use their language skills outside the classroom in real-life settings such as internships, residential language houses, or community outreach programs. Such components have been very beneficial to program visibility and to creating student interest in foreign language study at several institutions.

Those schools fortunate enough to have "language houses" have, of course, an optimal setting for involving students in realistic communication and in language and culture-related activities. A unique facility is the Oldenborg Center for Modern Languages and International Relations at Pomona College. The Center serves as a residential facility for students in five languages (Chinese, French, German, Russian, and Spanish), housed in different parts of the building, and supervised by native language residents. All rooms have access to the "Voice of Oldenborg," taped programs in the five languages that are prepared weekly by the residents. In addition to its residential function, Oldenborg Center offers a large range of activities to the total campus and to the Claremont community. For instance, every day at lunch time conversation groups meet in twenty different languages. Many center residents and other interested students and faculty from the five-college consortium at Claremont take advantage of this opportunity to practice their conversation skills. In addition to the "conversation tables," the center offers a wide variety of formal and informal activities relating to international and intercultural issues, including films, lectures, discussions, conferences, ethnic dinners, an international carnival, and other student planned and directed activities. Students, whether residing at Oldenborg Center or not, can earn academic credit for participating in the conversation groups and other activities sponsored by the center. Especially interesting is the fact that a large percentage of Oldenborg residents are not foreign language majors but students who want to develop or maintain fluency in a foreign language while majoring in other disciplines.[21]

Although the "Residential College" at the University of Michigan was not one of the programs visited in the follow-up study, the French House, which is a part of that experimental program, appears to fulfill functions similar to those performed by the Oldenborg Center at Pomona. The Michigan program is not multinational in scope, however; it offers courses and activities dealing with French language and culture only. One underlying concept of the Residential College is that students live and are taught in the same facilities. While the College offers no foreign language major as such, students must show proficiency by passing either an upper-level seminar or an interdisciplinary course actually taught in a language other than English. The French House at the University of Michigan offers a range of courses and opportunities for interaction with professors and speakers of French and has been mentioned as a factor contributing to program popularity.

The University of Southern California (USC) has developed a community service and outreach program called Joint Educational Project (JEP), in which students can earn partial course credit for participating in weekly field assignments that are an integral part of some regular college courses. Although JEP involves students in many fields, because of the large number of Spanish speakers in the Los Angeles community the program is particularly popular with students of Spanish who take advantage of the opportunity to practice their language skills with native Spanish speakers in bilingual schools. JEP Spanish students have served as bilingual aides to school nurses, taught minicourses in consumer education for Spanish speaking parents, taught minicourses in dental hygiene to elementary school children, served as aides to teachers in English as a Second Language (ESL) adult education courses and to teachers in bilingual elementary and junior high school programs, become "pals" to young students with special needs, and tutored individual youngsters with learning difficulties. Spanish is not the only language department participating in JEP. Classics students have taught minicourses on "Word Power" (Greek and Latin roots of words), and minicourses on Japanese heritage and the cultural background of other peoples are occasionally given on the high school level.

Although JEP has become an integral and popular component of many undergraduate Spanish courses, participation is optional. Multisection courses have JEP and non-JEP sections so that students may opt for or against a field experience. Even if no JEP sections are available, students can participate in

JEP in lieu of some other class requirement. JEP students spend from one to eight hours a week in the public schools or other public agencies. They are supervised and given help with planning their projects by their own college instructors, a community school teacher, or other resource person. According to JEP administrators, major benefits of the experience to university students are that they can "draw on materials and methodologies from their own courses and learn a subject through teaching it. In trying to make it interesting to younger students they gain a greater understanding of its relevance to themselves. The process of planning and working together helps reinforce learning for minicourse team members. It also provides an easy way to create small groupings of learners out of even the largest lecture class."[22]

USC, located in a vast urban community with a large population of Spanish speakers and large groups of ethnic minorities, offers an ideal setting for a community involvement program such as JEP. With some adaptation and imagination, the concept can also be utilized, though perhaps on a smaller scale, by other foreign language departments.

Recruiting, Publicizing, and Advising

If the past several years of falling enrollments have taught language teachers a lesson, it is that Madison Avenue techniques are useful not just for selling consumable goods but also for attracting students to the market of academic offerings. Practically all chairpersons consulted mentioned the importance of departmental visibility, of active recruiting of students, and of better communication with students, advisers, colleagues in other fields, administrators, and, of course, the public in general. Some exemplary programs involving the conscious and systematic use of publicity techniques are found at Slippery Rock State College[23] and Washington State University.

Some departments have developed attractive program brochures that explain the reasons and advantages of foreign language study and describe curricular offerings and how they might fit into a student's program. Such a brochure is sent to all incoming freshmen at Washington State University, for example. The same institution conducts career colloquia, inviting students in all fields to explain the value of knowing a foreign language for various professions and how language study can be combined with other major fields of study. Some departments provide students with detailed course descriptions listing content, objectives, instructional materials, assignments, and evaluation methods. These descriptions can also serve as sources of information for undergraduate advisors and area high school teachers.

Very few departments seem to make any systematic effort to inform area high school teachers of placement criteria and procedures. A notable exception is an effort by the Texas chapter of the American Association of Teachers of German (North Central Council, Dallas-Fort Worth area). This organization has established a committee of high school and university foreign language teachers for the purpose of coordinating a placement test that is currently being used by several area universities.[24]

Essentially departmental visibility means advertising and publicizing course offerings, efforts, and accomplishments. Often, a major reason for low enrollment in a special course or newly developed option is poor communication with those people who could most benefit from the option. Departmental visibility also involves conducting informational meetings for advisors, making an attempt to relate foreign language study to the rest of the curriculum. Such gatherings provide an opportunity for advisors to learn about program objectives and course requirements and to note a profile description of the type of student who can benefit most from a foreign language experience.

Maintaining good public relations means issuing news releases describing the activities of the faculty and the department in general, sponsoring lectures, films, festivals, fairs, summer or weekend immersion camps, theater performances, informal evening discussions, and soirées for folkdancing, singing, or ethnic cooking—and inviting the public to these events; it means obtaining and utilizing a share of program time on university radio and television stations; making translation services available to the community; and offering area high schools, social, or professional organizations a slate of departmental members who are willing to speak about foreign language or culture-related topics of general interest, or who will show film or slide presentations on some aspect(s) of a country. In short, as one chairperson summarized it: "We all have to become hustlers." Or, in the words of another: "We have to proselytize foreign languages with a missionary zeal."

4 | *DESCRIPTIONS OF SELECTED PROGRAMS*

This chapter contains descriptions of foreign language offerings at five different four-year institutions. Although the programs vary in size and methodology, they have experienced significant enrollment growth in foreign languages despite small gains in institutional enrollment.

Dartmouth College: Departments of Romance Languages, German, and Russian

Arriving at Dartmouth College, I was greeted rather unceremoniously by a gentleman completing a change of clothes from eighteenth-century costume back to twentieth-century attire after having taught a drama class. I met John Rassias, the originator of the Dartmouth Intensive Language Model, while he was simultaneously trying to tie his shoes, button his shirt, answer the telephone, and give instructions to a waiting student. A man of rare personal warmth, strong convictions, and a seemingly unlimited supply of energy, Rassias believes that ninety percent of instructional success is determined by instructor enthusiasm, and he appears to live and teach accordingly. Due, in part, to the efforts of Rassias, the modern foreign language programs at Dartmouth College have recently gained national attention for their innovative teaching methodology and success in developing second-language proficiency after a relatively short amount of time.[25] The romance language department (offering French, Italian, and Spanish majors) has had the most phenomenal success. The department compares with the English department in both size of faculty (30) and number of students enrolled. French is the largest section with approximately one half of the 4,000 students enrolled at Dartmouth taking French courses during their college career.

Dartmouth College is a small, private, co-educational (since 1972) liberal arts college in rural New Hampshire. While it offers a number of graduate programs in several disciplines, foreign languages are taught only on the undergraduate level. Dartmouth provides a uniquely supportive setting and motivation for foreign language study. It has a strong commitment to a liberal education, selective admission, a residential campus conducive to flexible scheduling patterns and experimental innovation, a student body that comes from predominantly upper-middle-class backgrounds and a majority of whom participate in programs abroad, a one-year (three-term) foreign language requirement for all students, as well as a four-course humanities distribution requirement that can be satisfied with a foreign language. But these external factors alone cannot explain the impressive growth during the period investigated. For instance, French increased by 140 students (36%) between fall 1972 and fall 1976; Italian increased by 50 students (new program); Spanish by 50 students (50%); and German by 113 students (66%)—all compared to an institutional enrollment growth of about 25%. Annual enrollment figures compare even more favorably. Only Russian showed a decline for the period investigated; however, it doubled its number of majors. (The decline in Russian enrollments may be due in part to the two years of preparatory study required before a student can go abroad. The other languages require only one or two terms of preliminary study.)

Teachers and administrators agreed that three factors account for the success and popularity of the departments visited: 1) a superior staff with high scholarly and teaching ability; 2) the Dartmouth Intensive Model (the only instructional option available for introductory language study); and 3) the many opportunities for language study abroad.

The Dartmouth Intensive Model is a two-term intensive sequence requiring approximately 2½ hours of instruction daily, five days per week, for the ten week terms. Students meet for one fifty-minute class period in a group of up to twenty-five students with a master teacher, who is a regular faculty member. In addition, they meet for one period in small groups of between five and ten students with an apprentice teacher (A.T.), a specially trained undergraduate student with adequate fluency in the language, who serves as drill instructor. An additional half hour's work is required for independent study in the language laboratory.

The scheduling problems that such an extended time block might cause are to a large extent overcome by offering the drill sections during times when few or no other classes are in session, for instance at eight o'clock in the morning, at noon, or at five in the afternoon. Since Dartmouth is predominantly a residential campus with relatively few students employed outside the institution, most students are able to fit one of these periods into their schedule. The master teachers' classes are offered throughout the day in the regular course plan; and laboratory practice is, of course, at the student's convenience.

The master teachers' classes provide the nucleus for the intensive model. Here, new vocabulary is presented, dialogues are introduced, grammatical and phonological features are explained, and insights into the target culture are provided. The master teachers differ in methodological approaches according to language and personality. French tends toward the exclusive use of the language in instruction while German and Russian make more frequent use of English in the classroom. Some instructors tend toward an audio-lingual orientation, others use a more direct methodology, and some are quite traditional, relying heavily on grammatical explanation and on translation.

The unifying feature (and perhaps the most innovative aspect) of the Dartmouth Model is the daily intensive drill sessions conducted by apprentice teachers. These A.T.'s are undergraduate students selected at the beginning of each term after a three-day training workshop on the basis of vitality, pronunciation and general language competence, enthusiasm, and demonstration of their ability as drill masters. Competition for these apprenticeships is keen. In French, for instance, up to four students compete for each available position. Occasionally, students "try out" several times before they are finally accepted. Students do not need to be language majors. In fact, more than half of the apprentice teachers interviewed were majoring in other disciplines, among them history, government, geography, English, and economics.

The sole function of these undergraduate assistants is conducting highly structured, strictly audio-lingual pattern drills to practice pronunciation and grammatical patterns. A.T.'s are discouraged from making grammatical explanations, giving extensive translations, or using English during the drill sessions. They are trained to use a lively, rapid-fire drill method, keeping students' attention by such practices as constantly moving among them, rhythmic finger snapping, and pointing to one student to respond while keeping eye contact with another student. Correct student responses are rewarded by prolific praise, ranging from happy smiles and pieces of candy to verbal and physical "pats on the back." (One "slow learner," after several wrong attempts, received a kiss from an apparently elated drill master when he finally completed his task correctly.) Incorrect responses earn frowns, oral reprimands, threatening gestures, and the tenacious attention of the A.T. until the error is corrected. Immediate error correction is an important feature of the method.

After being quite intimidated and frustrated by an enthusiastic A.T. who included me in Russian drill practice while I attended the drill session as an observer (I must admit, neither cajoling nor threats elicited the correct response), I expected to hear negative student reaction to the histrionics of the A.T.'s, the intense pressure to perform, the feeling of constantly being "on the spot," and the often exclusively mechanical practice of language patterns. But not one student among the many consulted (including entire classes without the presence of an instructor) reacted negatively to the procedures. While some students admitted that the drills were often purely mechanical in nature and the actual meaning of what was being said and practiced was not always clear, they saw such practice as a necessary component of language instruction. Students reacted especially positively to error correction and to the small size of the drill sessions, which forces every student to participate actively and gives each student extensive opportunities for individual response. Incidentally, a number of students mentioned that they were studying a second foreign language because of the positive experience with prior intensive study of another language. (The Hawthorne effect probably accounts to some extent for the unquestioningly positive attitudes of the student body. Most students are quite aware of the national attention the foreign language programs at Dartmouth have received and are accustomed to frequent visitors and observers to their classes.)

The use of undergraduate A.T.'s is the departments' best advertisement;

doubtless it has a positive psychological effect on beginning language students. Often these apprentice teachers are only one year ahead of the students they drill and thus can relate in a relaxed and unthreatening manner to their peers. But more important, the excellent language fluency and pronunciation of the A.T.'s serve as encouragement to the students, who see how little time separates them from their own painful beginnings and the impressive proficiency of the drill instructors. As already mentioned, the apprenticeships are highly coveted positions, partly because they provide some financial remuneration (A.T.'s receive minimum hourly wages for three hours per teaching day—one hour for the actual classroom contact and two hours for preparation time) and partly because the assignment provides the opportunity to use language skills and gives valuable experience in teaching techniques and in relating to students. Some openly admitted that serving as A.T.'s gave them prestige and ego support from the peers they were teaching.

The training and supervision of apprentice teachers are taken seriously. There are no set course prerequisites for students competing for A.T.-ships. In practice, however, all A.T.'s interviewed had spent a minimum of one term in the target language country. Because of the popularity of the A.T. positions, departments have established a rule that students cannot serve as drill masters for more than two terms. In addition to this limitation, each prospective drill master must repeat the training workshop and compete for the position at the beginning of each quarter he or she wishes to serve, regardless of prior experience.

While the initial training of A.T.'s is handled jointly for all languages at the beginning of each term, supervision during the term falls to the master teachers to whom the A.T.'s are assigned. In each language, A.T.'s have a joint weekly planning session. Also, master and apprentice teachers work together closely in weekly meetings, and apprentices are periodically observed and evaluated throughout the term by a number of different master teachers. Several professors mentioned the crucial importance of guidance and close supervision of the A.T.'s.

Attendance at language laboratory sessions is less rigorously enforced and less popular among students than is attendance at drill sessions. Student resistance to the lab is due to the already familiar complaints of inadequate or insufficient materials, inadequate pacing, lack of reinforcement, poor sound quality, and boredom in dealing with a machine. Essentially, the language laboratory and the A.T.-conducted drill periods have the same function; theoretically, at least, the lab should fulfill the task of drilling students. In practice, however, it is interaction with a lively, enthusiastic, and concerned human prompter that greatly enhances the appeal and success of the drill session. To overcome some of the shortcomings of the laboratory setting a set of video lab tapes is being developed that present a filmed version of a drill session in action. These videotapes attempt to enlist the active involvement of the viewer by soliciting a response each time the drill master on television points to an empty chair among the students he is working with in the film.

Among the languages taught in the Dartmouth Intensive Model, only French uses a set of specially developed instructional materials. All other languages have adapted commercially available textbooks and accompanying tape series. Satisfaction with materials is far from unanimous among instructors. As can be expected, much effort must go into preparing supplementary exercise and drill materials.

The introductory intensive courses are not the only successful language programs at Dartmouth. Upper-level foreign language programs at Dartmouth provide relatively traditional offerings consisting predominantly of literature and some culture and civilization courses as well as literature and culture courses in translation. Interest in upper-level work is quite strong and has increased in recent years since many students who return from an experience abroad wish to maintain their language skills and deepen their understanding of the culture they have experienced first hand. The A.T. system, of course, also serves as a means of maintaining the interest of students returning from study abroad; however, as is often the case with departments that have flourishing study abroad programs, chairpersons at Dartmouth expressed the difficulty of offering course work on a level and breadth that utilizes the knowledge students have acquired abroad.

As mentioned above, recent increases in the number of foreign language majors at Dartmouth have been impressive: French majors practically doubled between 1972 and 1976 (from 16 to 31 per class); Russian showed an increase (from 7 to 15) over the same time period; and Spanish increased its majors from 6 to 10. Only German shows a decline in majors (from 9 in 1972 to 5 in 1976). As appears to be the trend elsewhere, a larger number of students than in the past complete double majors or "modified majors" (an individually designed combination of a set number of courses in a foreign language and a supportive discipline lending itself to an interdisciplinary focus).

A strong factor contributing to the success of the Dartmouth language departments is the programs offering study abroad. Many students choose to complete their language requirement by spending at least one term in a foreign country after initial language study at Dartmouth. Before students can participate in a program in a country speaking a Romance language, they must take a minimum of one term of French, Spanish, or Italian. German requires two terms of prior language study, and Russian requires six terms before a student can study abroad. The extensive prerequisite preparation in Russian is believed to discourage some students from studying the language, but experience at Dartmouth and elsewhere has indicated that a minimum of two years of preliminary language study is needed before a student can function effectively in the Soviet Union. Despite this heavy prerequisite, at least half of the two dozen Dartmouth students who study at the University of Leningrad each summer are non-majors.

Dartmouth offers several types of overseas experiences: *Language Study Abroad* in Canada, France, Germany, Italy, Mexico, and Spain; *Foreign Study* in Austria, Central America (Costa Rica and Panama), England, France, Germany, Greece, Mexico, Italy, Russia, Scotland, Spain, and Sweden (these programs are sponsored jointly by the various language departments and the departments of music, earth sciences, biology, religion, English, philosophy, and geography); *Independent Study Programs* in Romania; and *Exchange Programs* with German universities and with Keio University in Japan. Obviously, the availability of these programs provides motivation for foreign language study not present in many other institutions. An informal survey revealed that more than half of the students in an introductory German course were planning to study in a German-speaking country. The prospect of needing the language as a means of survival within the next year certainly contributes significantly toward the motivation for language study. The study-abroad component also affects the availability of proficient undergraduate A.T.'s. Few undergraduates without an experience abroad would be able to display the fluency and mastery of the language demonstrated by Dartmouth A.T.'s.

Department chairpersons at Dartmouth emphasized the importance of a total departmental commitment to lower-level instruction. No division of assignment is made between junior and senior faculty. Everyone shares in lower-level language instruction, and the assignments to supervise and direct programs abroad are on a rotating basis. All staff interviewed agreed that the success of the program is based on concentrated efforts of each individual faculty member, including frequent willingness to carry an overload.

Because of the special setting and educational purposes of Dartmouth College, it is tempting to discount the Dartmouth experience as one that cannot be adapted to other institutions. True, student motivation toward language study is probably higher than at many other institutions because of family background, educational aims, and the likelihood of being able to use the language in a study-abroad setting. But the success at Dartmouth in terms of student achievement as well as in terms of program attractiveness is based on certain principles that apply to all foreign language instruction and that should not be ignored:

1) Extended daily exposure to the language. Common sense tells us that the more time one spends in learning a task, the quicker one masters it. (While comparative test scores are not systematically collected, student proficiency after only one term of study appears to be quite high.)

2) Daily small-group drill periods in which students intensively practice vocabulary and grammatical patterns to which they have been introduced during regular instruction. These small-group sessions permit high frequency individual responses (faculty estimated that each student responds an average of sixty-five times an hour).

3) High emphasis on oral work to meet the largely oral communicative objectives of the course and to prepare students for oral interaction in the target language country.

4) The use of undergraduate peers as drill masters to practice the language in a non-threatening setting and to demonstrate to students through the example of the drill instructor that the rewards of language study are not as remote as they might initially appear.

5) Lively, energetic, enthusiastic, fast-moving paraprofessionals providing intense interpersonal contact and displaying human concern, humor, and intense preoccupation with student success in mastering the language tasks practiced. (Observers of drill sessions occasionally react negatively to the theatrics of A.T.'s. While pivoting, rhythmic finger snapping, expansive gestures, climbing on furniture, and so forth are probably not essential to the success of the drill sessions, a certain "choreography" is necessary to keep a fast-moving rhythm, in order to maintain student interest and participation, and to avoid the boredom inherent in long periods of manipulative language practice. Also, A.T.'s need some specific techniques and methodological guidelines to set the pace, convey enthusiasm, and maintain the high frequency interaction crucial to the success of the drill sessions.)

Schools providing fewer opportunities to study abroad or schools with a student body financially less privileged than Dartmouth's might not have a large pool of capable students to serve as drill leaders. Since the small-group intensive drill sessions are predominantly manipulative and do not require flawless fluency on the part of the leader, some additional training and intensive language preparation before each drill session could prepare advanced undergraduate language students at other institutions for this assignment. In addition, graduate students and native speakers from the community could be recruited for the drill assignment.

The Dartmouth Model is rather expensive because of the large-scale use of paid A.T.'s. (Incidentally, the Exxon foundation has absorbed most of the A.T. cost through a grant and is considering applications by other institutions for funds to develop similar programs.) The cost factor in utilizing undergraduate drill leaders does not need to be prohibitive; instead of monetary rewards, students could be given academic credit for their service. Departments preparing foreign language teachers could use the apprenticeships as valuable internships that might even become a program requirement for teacher preparation.

For more information on the Dartmouth Intensive Language Model, including a film developed with a grant from the Exxon Foundation, write

> Professor John A. Rassias
> Department of Romance Languages and Literatures
> Dartmouth College
> Hanover, New Hampshire 03755.

For general program information and the application of the Intensive Language Model to the various languages write

> Professor David Sices, Chairman
> Department of Romance Languages and Literatures
> Dartmouth College
> Hanover, New Hampshire 03755

> Professor Steven P. Scher, Chairman
> Department of German
> Dartmouth College
> Hanover, New Hampshire 03755

> Professor Richard R. Sheldon, Chairman
> Department of Russian Language and Literature
> Dartmouth College
> Hanover, New Hampshire 03755.

The Middlebury College Language Schools

Any visitor who gets lost on the Middlebury campus during the summer should seek directions from middle-aged individuals. While this is no guarantee that the wanderer will find a sympathetic soul who will point out the right direction (Middlebury summer students come in all age categories), the chances of finding someone willing to use his or her mother tongue are greater. My own experiences illustrate the frustration (or delight, if one happens to understand the language being spoken) that the Middlebury language pledge can cause: I was looking for a particular Russian class for which my schedule indicated the building but not the room number. After asking a young man for help in English I was returned a stream of "gibberish" of which only the initial *da* was comprehensible. I indicated that, unfortunately, I did not speak Russian and asked him to please direct me to my classroom in a common medium. Again I received a lengthy incomprehensible exposé (this time very slowly and with much gesticulation), whereupon I took the young man's arm and threatened to hang on until he led me to the desired location. He then silently walked me up four flights of stairs and delivered me to my destination, again with much gibberish to the instructor and to the general amusement of the class. Perhaps not every Middlebury student takes the language pledge as seriously as the young man in question, but the incident gives some indication of the motivation and commitment that many students bring to their summer study.

The renowned summer language program at Middlebury College forms a special category among the programs visited. One of the factors that brought me to the campus was my curiosity about the discrepancy between a growing summer program and a regular academic-year program that appeared to suffer from some of the same pains as foreign language departments elsewhere, at least as far as enrollments are concerned. I found, however, that the regular academic year and the summer school are independent of each other (though apparently well articulated) and that success in one program in terms of student interest does not necessarily assure success in the other since the two programs function under quite different constraints.

Before 1973, Middlebury had established a reputation mainly for its graduate programs (M.A. and D.M.L.) in modern foreign languages and teacher training. The undergraduate summer program in the western languages is only five years old. (Chinese has been taught since 1966 and Japanese since 1970.) From an enrollment of 290 students in undergraduate summer programs in 1973, the number of students climbed to 400 in 1977. At present, Chinese, French, German, Italian, Japanese, Spanish, and Russian can be studied on the lower levels, and plans are under way to add Arabic.

The undergraduate summer program is an intensive immersion program of seven weeks' duration (nine weeks for Russian and East Asian languages) requiring a daily minimum of three to four hours of class contact, plus practice in the laboratory, for six credit hours (ten hours for Chinese, Japanese, and Russian). In addition to the regularly scheduled class time, Middlebury students have practically unlimited opportunity to hear and speak their selected language out of class in language-specific dormitories and dining rooms and at formal and informal gatherings offering films, concerts, recitals, lectures, slide presentations, poetry readings, theater performances, discussions, sing alongs, picnics, sports competitions, and more. Since the graduate and undergraduate courses run simultaneously, a large number of fluent speakers of the various languages are available.

A well-known feature of the program is the Middlebury language pledge requiring students to sign a promise to use exclusively the language they are studying while they are on campus. As indicated above, the pledge is apparently taken rather seriously. Furthermore, instruction is almost totally in the foreign language. Only in Russian and in the East Asian languages did I hear an occasional English explanation or translation in introductory classes.

The undergraduate program structure and enrollment patterns differ to some extent from language to language. While Chinese, German, Italian, Japanese, and Russian have relatively large introductory enrollments, French and Spanish have larger enrollments on the intermediate and third-year levels. (Fourth-year undergraduate language instruction was added in 1978.) For the sake of efficiency, the following curricular description is a general one.

The methodology used by the various languages is quite eclectic. Apart from the exclusive use of the target language as medium of instruction, instructors are free to follow their own methodological inclinations, ranging from a modified audio-lingual approach (depending heavily on pattern drills), to direct methodology (inductive question and answer technique), to an analytical, cognitive, grammar-oriented approach. In Italian and German lower-level classes, there is heavy use of visual materials. Italian uses the Didier Audio-Visual Method and the textbook *Parola e Pensiero* by Vincenzo Traversa (New York: Harper & Row, 1976). Especially noteworthy is a set of German television commercials, accompanied by written texts and exercises developed by Middlebury faculty. These authentic videotapes appear quite effective in holding student interest. Unfortunately, because of copyright laws, the materials cannot yet be made available commercially.

A student's daily schedule generally consists of four hours of classroom instruction and one hour of language lab practice. Classroom work includes large-group grammar explications, presentation of audio-visual materials, discussion of reading assignments, and small-group drill and communication practice. Instructors and classrooms change frequently to avoid monotony and boredom and to expose students to different idiolects.

Biweekly quizzes are corrected and returned within a day of administration (some instructors work as teams to correct them while others continue teaching). In addition to frequent short quizzes, students are given a final comprehensive examination. Some of the languages also administer an appropriate form of the MLA Cooperative Foreign Language and/or CLEP tests as pre- and post-tests to compare student performance with national norms. Middlebury students score very highly on all parts of the four-skill tests.

The intermediate level includes a comprehensive grammar review and stresses composition and conversation. In German, students can choose two minicourses (or modules) according to their linguistic abilities and individual interests during each half of the summer term. Options include reading selections from various authors, readings from the press (journalistic writings), readings from the humanities or social sciences, or readings dealing with cultural aspects of German speaking countries. Students can also work on translation skills.

The third-year program follows a pattern similar to that of the intermediate program, but students have a wider selection of individual interest options. Options during summer 1977 included a workshop on "The Art of

Cabaret," a translation workshop, and modules on "Perspectives on Modern Germany" and "Advanced Readings: Selections from Günther Grass and Thomas Mann." Students working on the same module are given opportunities to interact in small groups. (For a more detailed description of the German program see Gerd K. Schneider, "Final Report on the Undergraduate Language Program at Middlebury College. Summer 1975," ERIC/CLL. ED 116 464; "Final Report. . . . Summer 1976," ERIC/CLL. ED 134 030; "A Model for a Successful Summer Foreign Language Program in German," *ADFL Bulletin*, 8, No. 4 [1977], 27–29.)

What factors then are the "key" to Middlebury's success in terms of attracting students to its summer language schools and in terms of student achievement? Administrators, staff, and students mentioned a number of contributing factors, including the purpose, setting, and constraints of the summer language schools:

(1) An outstanding team of instructors with a wide range of personalities and teaching styles works closely together in daily planning and implementation. A major factor of success in the eyes of program administrators is flexibility in staffing. The summer language schools use largely non-tenured faculty from a number of institutions nationwide as well as from abroad. This practice permits year-to-year curricular changes and the offering of new and unique courses by hiring specialists in fields where need is most acute. In other words, program offerings are not limited to the specialties and interests of resident faculty, but can draw on national and international expertise.

(2) The student body is highly motivated. Some have concrete plans to spend time in the country whose language they are learning; others hope to relate language skills to specific career goals ranging from archeology and art history to comparative literature, international law and business, medicine, music, political science, or psychology; still others hope to fulfill a language requirement at their home institutions without making the usual time commitment of from two to four semesters. Many students come from prestigious private or state institutions and are accustomed to rigorous work and high expectations. Some of the students have already graduated and are established in various careers.

(3) The intensive exposure (up to five hours of formal instruction per day, as well as the many opportunities for extracurricular activities conducted in the language) and the language pledge provide a setting for total linguistic immersion. This factor surely contributes to the high percentile ranking achieved by Middlebury summer students on the MLA Cooperative and CLEP tests. While students receive only six hours of academic credit (ten hours for Chinese, Japanese, and Russian) for their summer work, the number of contact hours with the language is enormous when compared with contact hours in a traditional foreign language program.

(4) A high student/faculty ratio facilitates small-group instruction and interaction and permits much individual attention. (For instance, total undergraduate enrollment in German in the summer of 1977 was 79: 32 in first-year; 25 in second-year; and 22 in third-year German. The full-time undergraduate faculty numbered seven, plus two part-time and several guest lecturers.)

(5) Many of the teachers live on campus in the same dormitories as the students. This proximity provides literally around-the-clock opportunities for

formal and informal contact. Faculty members regularly take all meals with the students in language-specific dining rooms and participate in the same out-of-class activities as the students, from playing soccer, volleyball, and tennis to participating in meditation exercises.

(6) Weekly program evaluation sessions by students make staff aware of problems as they arise and permit changes and adaptations throughout the term.

(7) The long history (starting in 1915 with the German School) and outstanding reputation of the Middlebury graduate summer programs attract many students from all parts of the country. Several students mentioned that they selected Middlebury because of the experiences and recommendations of friends who had participated in the language schools previously.

(8) The number of graduate students enrolled in the graduate summer programs provides willing helpers and "conversers."

(9) The Middlebury setting, a lovely, small-town campus that is utilized only by the language schools during the summer, contributes to the success by permitting the isolation necessary for linguistic immersion.

The academic-year program at Middlebury College is relatively traditional, focusing on language, literature, and civilization. The undergraduate lower-division language courses are still taught semi-intensively, requiring generally six contact hours per week (three large-group lectures and three small-group practice sessions plus lab work) for three hours of academic course credit.

Middlebury is moving in the direction of offering "extended majors," in which foreign languages are studied as supportive skills for various disciplines. An extended major can be acquired by participating in the junior year abroad in any of the five affiliated institutions in Florence, Madrid, Mainz, Moscow, and Paris. Study abroad is an integral component of the Middlebury curriculum; a large percentage of students from all fields of study participate. The challenge faced by foreign language departments at Middlebury and other institutions with well-developed and heavily subscribed foreign study programs is to develop courses and options that attract students returning to campus from an extended stay in another country.

For more information write

> Professor Roger M. Peel
> Director of the Language Schools
> Middlebury College
> Middlebury, Vermont 05753.

Ohio State University: Department of Classics

The Department of Classics at Ohio State University (OSU) has had an appreciable enrollment increase in its Latin and classics programs in the recent past. Only Greek has shown a decline. Annual enrollments in Latin courses increased 66% (385 students) between 1974 and 1976; in classics courses, enrollments increased 28% (905 students) for the same period. The overall undergraduate institutional growth for these years has been only 6% (2,147 students).

The department offers five areas of concentration for majors: 1) Classical Humanities (Greek and Latin classical works in translation); 2) Greek; 3) Latin; 4) Greek and Latin; and 5) Classical Languages and Ancient History, offered in cooperation with the history department. The teaching staff consists of 14 full-time faculty (two more positions than in 1972) and 25 graduate teaching assistants.

OSU has a twenty-quarter-hour (four quarters) language requirement for students in the combined colleges of the Arts and Sciences, affecting approximately forty percent of the total undergraduate enrollment. The requirement has not been modified in the recent past. Since it can be satisfied by language courses in any of the languages offered at OSU, it is in itself no major reason for the large enrollment increases in the classics department.

Several reasons were cited for having contributed to the department's impressive growth. Repeated mention was made of a renewed interest in Latin and classical antiquity—apparently a national phenomenon noted by several other classics departments participating in the study. The acting chairman, Charles Babcock, credited an outstanding and committed teaching staff that is active in course development and willing to try innovative approaches. Three programs in particular have had a positive effect on enrollment trends: 1) the development of an individualized (self-paced) study option for the first three courses in the introductory Latin sequence (Latin 101, 102, and 103); 2) the addition to the curriculum of a multimedia (slide-tape), partially audio-tutorial mythology course; and 3) a computer-assisted course in medical terminology. The three programs are discussed below.

In 1975, OSU implemented a self-paced Latin option for a three-course Latin sequence. Student response, as reflected in enrollment figures and decreased attrition rates between courses, has been very favorable. The individualized option uses essentially the same materials as the traditional classroom option: *Cambridge Latin Course* (Cambridge University Press, 1975) together with *Elementary Latin: A Self-Paced Course*, developed by Dennis M. Kratz, Douglas N. Lacey, and Judith D. Lawson of the OSU staff. Students are permitted to switch from the individualized option to the traditional option and vice versa at various points during the quarter. Quite a few students make the change each quarter, predominantly from the traditional classroom to the individualized option. The individualized option differs from the traditional option in three respects: 1) self-pacing, 2) the expectation of an eighty percent mastery level for passing, and 3) the availability of variable credit.

The individualized Latin option is essentially a self-paced independent study program in that it enables students to work where, when, and as much (or as little) as they please. During the first two weeks of the quarter, students registered for the individualized option meet as a class. Here they learn the procedures and constraints of the course, become familiar with the materials and facilities, and are guided through the first learning module as a group. After this initiation, students make use of the Latin Individualized Learning Center (a large resource room with attached testing facilities) at their convenience. This study center is open during regular university hours and (depending on the time of the day) is operated continuously by up to three staff members. Duties are shared by graduate teaching assistants and regular faculty, who provide individual help, answer student queries, and administer, supervise, and correct unit tests. Essentially, the students work independently or with a partner through instructional materials that give step-by-step guidance for activities and exercises to be completed for each unit. Students come to the study/testing center whenever they want a worksheet corrected, when they have questions, or when they feel they have mastered the materials and are ready to take a unit test. All testing is done in the Latin Individualized Learning Center. Since tests are corrected immediately by a staff member, students receive an instant evaluation of their performance; the staff member can discuss errors with the student and make suggestions for dealing with remaining difficulties.

Students opting for the individualized Latin course must pass each unit exam at an eighty percent mastery level before they can receive credit for the unit and continue to the next. Those students not able to earn the minimum score on the first try may retake a form of the unit test as often as necessary until they reach the required mastery. In essence, the conventional *A* to *F* grading scale becomes an *A/B* scale since achievement below the *B* level is disregarded and does not appear on the student's record. There is, of course, a failing grade, but it is reserved for those students who make no provision to fulfill or readjust their contractual obligation for a set number of credit hours.

Since the individualized option is fully self-paced, students may adjust the number of credit hours to which they commit themselves during any one quarter. Each unit of the instructional materials carries one quarter hour of academic credit, which the student receives only after passing a final unit exam with a score equivalent to *80%* or above. Initially, all students register for five quarter hours, but during the seventh week of the term students review their progress with an adviser and may adjust their credits if they have either over- or underestimated the amount of time it takes to reach mastery level. Students then sign a credit contract, committing themselves to a set number of units to be completed during the quarter.

This variable credit arrangement permits a student to earn up to fifteen hours of credit during a quarter. If the contracted number of credits is not completed, the student receives an *incomplete* for the unfinished units and is given six weeks to complete them. If this deadline is not met, the student will receive a failing grade for those units he or she contracted but did not complete at an eighty percent mastery level.

While the individualized instruction wave that seemed to sweep the nation's college campuses during the early 1970s appears to have slowed down and while many departments that experimented with individualized instruction report a return to a traditional classroom approach, the classics department at OSU seems to have overcome many of the constraints that caused failure of individualized programs at other institutions. Based on the apparently successful experiment with Latin courses, five modern foreign languages (Arabic, French, German, Russian, and Spanish) are in the process of developing and implementing individualized introductory options with the support of a grant from the National Endowment for the Humanities. It will be interesting to note whether these additional options detract from the popularity of the individualized Latin courses and how successful they are in incorporating an effective oral component with opportunities for student interaction.

Faculty members, teaching assistants, and students at OSU expressed several concerns that are worth restating here for those departments considering development of similar options. The major concern of some faculty members is whether the individualized option can build as solid a foundation in the language as can the traditional classroom option. They fear that the division of course content into discrete units and the lack of a comprehensive final examination encourage "cramming" and memorization for a unit test, the contents to be forgotten after an acceptable score is achieved. Concern was expressed that the lack of opportunity for the spontaneous interaction that is offered in a traditional classroom setting can limit a student's development and full comprehension and synthesis of the materials presented. Some instructors mentioned their feeling that students from the individualized option who continue with traditional Latin study in the fourth (non-individualized) course of the introductory sequence are not so well prepared as students who have studied Latin in the traditional classroom option. Furthermore, there appears to be a retention problem. Unfortunately, although both options use the same syllabus, no data have yet been collected on test scores to compare achievement of students coming from the traditional and individualized options. The problem is, of course, that comparative end-of-term scores are difficult to obtain because of the variable time and credit elements and the retest possibility offered by the individualized course. Students from either option could be given a "one-shot" comprehensive final exam at the time they complete work for the five-credit-hour course, or they could be given a comprehensive review test when entering the next course in the sequence, especially the conventional fourth course in the series. Apart from serving as a measure of quality control, such a test could also be used as a diagnostic instrument to isolate deficiencies that must be remedied in order to assure student success at more advanced levels.

The problem of comparing the achievement of students from individualized and traditional course options is not unique to OSU. For instance, at the University of California at Berkeley, where individualized options have been offered in German and Italian for several years, some members of the teaching staff express similar apprehensions, particularly concerning the oral fluency of students coming from individualized courses. (Since oral fluency is not an objective of the OSU Latin program, this factor is not an appropriate criterion for judging the success of the program.)

Another area of concern not unique to the classics department of OSU is the need for a dependable screening process to predict probable success or aptitude for either the individualized or the traditional learning options. Self-paced study requires high motivation, independence, self-discipline, and refined study skills not possessed by every student, especially since an estimated ninety-five percent of the students take Latin to fulfill a requirement for graduation.

Materials, also a source of some dissatisfaction, can be a major problem with any individualized program. Few instructional series are available that do not need extensive adaption for use in self-paced learning. Any change in instructional materials will require an extensive commitment of time, energy, and money to develop a new set of independent learning units.

Concerns expressed by teaching assistants who have major responsibilities for staffing the Latin Individualized Study Center echoed to some extent those of regular faculty. Some considered their duties as tutors boring and lacking in challenge and expressed a preference for teaching a conventional class in which they could interact with students on a daily basis, have an active hand in structuring and directing learning, and have a chance to "grow with the materials." (In the Learning Center, tutors need to be totally familiar with the entire set of materials used in the individualized option since they work with students who are at various points in the introductory sequence.)

All students interviewed were generally quite positive about their experience. Some of them had studied Latin in high school and found the individualized option an efficient means of reviewing and completing the course at their convenience. The students liked the flexible time arrangement the individualized option permits and, especially, the fact that no oral performance is required in the course. (Incidentally, this factor was mentioned as a major reason for choosing Latin over a modern foreign language.) Student concerns, apart from an occasional complaint that tutorial help was not always available when needed, involved their own inability to discipline themselves to commit the necessary time and to work without stringent deadlines. They admitted that "Latin usually comes last" since other course work takes priority because of day-to-day assignments and scheduled exams.

While the self-paced option in Latin is more popular at OSU than the traditional one, individualized instruction is no panacea for all students at all stages, as the staff members in charge of the individualized program in the classics department are the first to admit. Many students do not complete the contracted amount of work, and most students cover less rather than more material per quarter—and earn fewer credits—than students in the traditional classroom. Contrary to the early rhetoric of the individualized instruction movement, failure is indeed possible. Self-paced instruction is not the route for every student; perhaps it is not even the way for the majority, once the newness of the program has worn off. But it is definitely a viable option that meets the needs of many students, as the OSU Latin model appears to indicate.

The second OSU option that is popular with students is a multimedia, partially audio-tutorial classical mythology course taught in English. While the course is not totally self-paced (students attend regularly scheduled large-group lectures and are required to take examinations at specified times in order to complete the course within the constraints of the academic quarter), students have free use of the Classical Humanities Learning Center to study the well-developed and coordinated slide/tape materials that make up a major part of the course materials. The Classical Humanities Learning Center (separate from the Latin Individualized Learning Center) is operated continuously by a member of the teaching staff who is able to give individual help when needed.

The facilities available to the classics department deserve special mention. The department is located in a newly constructed building with facilities designed to meet instructional needs (envious colleagues from the modern language departments at OSU refer to the quarters occupied by the classics department as "the Hilton" of the language departments). There are two separate learning centers for individual study. One is utilized predominantly by the individualized Latin program. The other is equipped with twenty-six individual study carrels (each with slide projector and tape recorder) that make it suited to the partially self-paced audio-tutorial approach of the classical mythology courses.

The terminology course is the third "major attraction" for students. Entitled "Classical Background of Scientific Terminology," it carries three credit hours and is basically designed as a career-supportive course for students preparing for health-related fields. Within the time constraints of the regular academic quarter, the course is essentially self-paced and uses computer-assisted instruction (CAI). The students work with the programmed materials at any computer terminal at their own convenience. Frequent self-testing and review are part of the course. Students must make a certain minimum score on a computer administered quiz before they can move on to the next unit. If they do not achieve the minimum score, they are given instructions for review and are automatically signed off.

The course consists of eighteen units dealing with etymology, base forms, affixes, word segmentation, terminology for the various anatomical systems, pharmaceutical abbreviations, colors, numbers, biological and zoological terms, and general terms of Latin and Greek origin that the students might encounter in their readings. Evaluation of students is based on two conventional tests (mid-term and final) scheduled several times throughout the quarter, thus permitting students to finish the course at various points during the term if they so desire. Optional discussion and pronunciation sessions are also scheduled during the quarter. The instructor in charge of the course is available for individual help when necessary.

The terminology course has an enrollment of approximately three hundred students per quarter. The instructor who developed the course reports little negative reaction to computer-assisted instruction after the students are initiated into its use. One of the major advantages of this form of instruction is that the program requires minimal instructor time once the course is developed, thus freeing instructors for individual assistance. Furthermore, the step-by-step progression of the programmed materials provides opportunities for constant reinforcement and review and permits flexible instruction time. (For a more detailed description, see Joseph R. Tebben, "VERBA: A Computer-Assisted Course in Terminology," *The Classical World*, Feb. 1975, pp. 299–304.)

Further information can be obtained from the following individuals: the self-paced Latin option, Dennis M. Kratz; the classical mythology course, John T. Davis; the computer-assisted terminology course, Joseph R. Tebben. All are members of the Department of Classics, Ohio State University, Columbus, Ohio 43210.

State University College at Buffalo: Foreign Language Department

The foreign language department at State University College at Buffalo (SUCB) shows an impressive enrollment increase (40% or 446 students versus only a 16% or 1,154 student increase in total institutional undergraduate enrollment) over the past four years. All languages except Latin have benefited from the influx of students; growth ranges from approximately 13% in German and Russian to 100% in Hebrew, with healthy increases in Italian (67%), Spanish and Polish (both 46%), and French (14%).

The department offers undergraduate degrees with majors only in French, German, Italian, and Spanish. Lower-division instruction is also available in

Hebrew, Polish, Russian, ESL, and Portuguese on a self-study basis. Despite increased departmental loads (fall 1972 enrollments—1,110; fall 1976 enrollments—1,556), the number of faculty positions decreased from 19 to 16¼ over the four-year period. To handle this additional burden, departmental teaching loads were increased voluntarily to four three-hour course sections per semester rather than maintaining the three-course load common in many other departments at SUCB.

The institution has a language requirement of twelve semester hours (four courses) for B.A. degree students only. The requirement, while essentially unchanged in number of credit hours, was modified in 1970 to permit the application of language as well as literature or culture in translation, linguistics, and ethnic studies courses toward fulfillment of the requirement. Furthermore, the department instituted a liberal transfer policy counting each year of high school foreign language study toward the language requirement without a verifying exam.

While the change in the foreign language requirement initially had a negative effect on enrollments in language courses, enrollment in newly developed "options" courses compensated for the loss, enabling traditional major programs in the department to be maintained. While other institutions responding to the survey also mentioned options courses as saving the language department from extinction, the initial survival efforts at SUCB have become a boon to traditional language courses by drawing attention to the department, providing departmental visibility, and thus improving community relations. Furthermore, these courses have contributed to the professional growth of many faculty by enabling them to develop new interests and subspecializations. Although the number of graduating majors in French and German has decreased since 1972, enrollments in the majority of language courses, especially at the lower levels, are higher than ever. This impressive growth cannot be attributed to one particular course, program, or language; it is due to a host of interacting and interrelated factors, all of which might come under the common heading of program diversification and visibility. Mandatory evaluation of teaching by students and peers may also have contributed.

The department has developed many popular options courses, including French, German, Italian Renaissance, modern Italian, Polish (and Polish Literature in Exile), Russian, Spanish, and Yiddish literatures in translation. Some special themes courses using a comparative approach (e.g., "Literature, Civilization, and Insanity") are offered jointly with the English department and are open to lower-division students. Contemporary culture courses, taught in English, deal with the cultures of France and Latin American countries. Since SUCB is essentially an urban campus whose constituency includes large ethnic populations with Italian, Jewish, Polish, and German backgrounds, courses such as "Italian-Americans: Literature and Society," "Spanish Composition for Native Speakers," and the respective language skills and literature in translation courses attract a sizable number of students and engender good community relations. (For a more detailed description of the ethnic studies course offerings, see Neil Rudin, "An Ethnic Studies Component in the Foreign Language Curriculum," *ADFL Bulletin*, 8, No. 2 [1976], 42–44.) Particularly popular options courses are a course on Greek and Roman mythology and an "Introduction to Language" course treating basic principles of linguistics, language universals, and language learning.

One curricular change that, in the opinion of some faculty members, contributed to enrollment growth was the change from a mandatory period in the departmental language lab (as a fourth contact hour for a three-credit course) to optional lab attendance in the Learning Resource Center. It appears that more students are willing to register for a foreign language if class-time commitments do not exceed those required by other academic disciplines. Because of the reduction in contact hours, the traditional first-year content of language courses is now spread over three semesters, a factor that has increased retention in the lower-division courses. Also, Spanish in particular is emphasizing oral communication skills in introductory courses to which students react quite favorably.

The foreign language teacher education component, which is especially well developed at SUCB, also deserves mention. The professional preparation of foreign language teachers is handled within the department and, apart from the traditional methods course, offers students extensive supervised experiences in the public schools with two student teaching assignments, one in an urban and one in a suburban setting. The department is in the process of implementing a competency based teacher education program.

For further information, write

Dr. Gisèle Feal, Chairperson
Foreign Language Department
State University College of New York
1300 Elmwood Avenue
Buffalo, New York 14222.

Washington State University: Department of Foreign Languages and Literatures

One might think of half a dozen reasons why Washington State University (WSU) should not be among the schools with a large enrollment increase in foreign languages. Located in a small town economically dependent on academe and agriculture, WSU is relatively isolated from major population centers and lacks many of the resources traditionally believed beneficial and supportive to a foreign language program. Yet, the Department of Foreign Languages and Literatures had an increase in student enrollments of over 26% (359 students) between fall 1972 and fall 1976 (versus an overall institutional growth of only 14%, or 1,831 students). Enrollment statistics are still more impressive if one goes back to 1970. Since then, foreign language enrollments have increased 53%. All languages show increased enrollments since 1972, ranging from 8% in French to 100% in Chinese, with the largest numerical increase in Spanish (203 students, or 61%).

The department offers majors in French, German, Spanish, and Russian; minors in the same languages as well as in Italian; and introductory and intermediate-level courses in Chinese, Japanese, Swedish, Swahili, Hindi, Sanskrit, Latin, and Greek. It also offers an M.A. in French, German, and Spanish and a Ph.D. in literary studies, sponsored jointly with the English department. The teaching staff at WSU consists of 21 full-time faculty (only ½ position more than in 1972, despite the large student increase) and 15 teaching assistants (versus 12 in 1972).

WSU has a one-year (eight semester hours) undergraduate entrance requirement for all students in the Division of Arts and Sciences (about sixty percent of the student population). This requirement is automatically fulfilled by two years of foreign language study at the high school level. Those students with no or insufficient foreign language background can fulfill the requirement only by traditional language courses. The foreign language requirement has not changed recently, and there is no intention of modifying it in the near future.

During my two-day visit to the campus, I visited several courses in session and talked to a cross section of professors representing all languages taught, to teaching assistants, to graduate and undergraduate students, and to administrators. It is difficult to point to one particular cause, course, program, method, or curricular innovation as being responsible for the department's success in attracting and maintaining student enrollments. Course offerings and methodologies are relatively traditional. Yet, the highly committed, cooperative faculty and dynamic departmental leadership have effected many "small" changes that have increased student enrollments. External factors have also contributed to growing interest in foreign language study. An overall institutional rise in enrollments, a strong commitment to and support of the liberal arts despite an emphasis on technical and agricultural fields in the major curriculum, a decrease in foreign language offerings in area high schools (which affects the number of students in requirement courses), an expanding Spanish speaking population (contributing to an awareness of the need for and benefits of foreign language study), a supportive administration that values the contribution of the department—all are factors that might have contributed directly or indirectly to the enrollment increase. Since most of these factors are beyond the direct control of the foreign language department, the following paragraphs will focus on those curricular components and procedures that were instituted through direct departmental efforts and that were cited repeatedly as having had some effect on program growth.

Accessibility of the faculty and leadership by the department chairman were two of the most frequently mentioned reasons for program success. WSU has a vertical teaching structure, utilizing senior faculty at all levels of language instruction. Faculty members are enthusiastic, highly accessible, willing to give extensive, individual attention, and strongly committed to undergraduate teaching. The chairman is an excellent organizer who uses every opportunity to bring his department to the attention of students and the public.

The addition of courses in less commonly taught languages (Chinese, Japanese, Swahili, Hindi, Sanskrit, Greek, and Swedish) also appears to have contributed to the overall enrollment. While some educators argue that a large choice of languages decreases enrollments in the more commonly taught languages, this does not seem to have been the case at WSU. Students attracted to the study of the less popular languages appear to be a rather specialized lot with particular goals and interests.

If one curricular innovation merits special mention for attracting students, affecting attitudes toward foreign language study, and improving student achievement, it is the intensive summer program. Originally begun in German and intended primarily as a quick means for graduate students to fulfill their language requirement, intensive summer courses are now offered in French,

German, Japanese, and Spanish and are open to all students, including high school seniors, regardless of language background. The courses offer two years of language instruction in eight weeks. Taught by teams of faculty and teaching assistants, students are involved in seven hours of structured and well-coordinated daily activities, ranging from explanations of grammar and drill groups to viewing slides, playing games, and singing. The intensive course satisfies the language requirement for undergraduates and for students in most graduate programs and helps foreign language majors to learn a second language without investing inordinate amounts of time. It also permits majors in other disciplines to acquire language skills that may be used in their professions.

Students who had started foreign language study at WSU in intensive summer courses and who were continuing their language study with third-year courses during the regular school year spoke positively of their summer experience in terms of language learning as well as "having had fun" and having established close personal relationships with faculty members and other students. They did not feel disadvantaged vis-à-vis classmates who had studied the language for two years in traditional courses. (For a more detailed description, the interested reader should see the following articles: David P. Benseler and Gertrud S. Mazur, "A New Approach to Language Learning for Graduate Students," *Modern Language Journal*, 57 [Sept.–Oct. 1973], 259–62; and David P. Benseler, "Increasing Upper Division Language Enrollment through Intensive Language Learning," *Foreign Language Annals*, 11 [Sept. 1978], 415–19.)

While no dependable statistics are available, students who have participated in the intensive summer courses appear to be more interested in continuing language study at advanced levels than are students who began their language study in traditional classes. Of course, those students willing to commit themselves to such summer immersion courses might be more strongly motivated to begin with than students who populate lower-division courses merely to fulfill a requirement.

In addition to courses in the less commonly taught languages and the summer intensive program, WSU offers an extensive choice of literature in translation courses, surveys of national literatures (e.g., "African Literature in English"), period or genre courses, and special topic or theme courses. The literature in translation courses may be applied toward a six-hour general arts and humanities requirement (the WSU catalogue lists a number of courses offered by other departments that may also be applied to the requirement, however).

The university provides several opportunities for students to develop language skills outside of class. Some out-of-class activities, while traditionally considered "extracurricular," have become part of the formal offerings, and students receive academic credit for active participation. For instance, the German choir (one credit hour) is open to all interested students regardless of language background. It meets once a week and performs frequently on and off campus. Participating students report consistent improvement in pronunciation and enjoy the immediate rewards of being able to "perform in German" as well as the fellowship the choir offers. The "French Cabaret," another out-of-class activity, performs a play in French once a semester and likewise offers one hour of credit for active participation. Students may also receive credit for regular attendance and participation in the "deutsche Mittagessen," a weekly conversation group. In addition, "la maison française" offers residential facilities for students interested in actively practicing their language skills and living in a French atmosphere.

Apart from the extracurricular programs that offer optional credit, all major languages offer one-hour conversation courses on the third-year level. Conducted by teaching assistants who are native speakers of the respective languages, these courses can be repeated up to four times for credit. The courses attract language majors who need to pick up "an extra hour" or so and non-majors with some formal or informal background in the languages who want to increase, maintain, and practice their language skills.

One of WSU's strong points is a sophisticated advising procedure, including a departmental career-counseling service. While no special career-related courses are offered apart from the traditional offerings for the B.A. or B.S. degrees, the department has placed one faculty member in charge of career counseling. Each semester, a colloquium is provided to inform all interested students, not just language majors, of career possibilities utilizing foreign languages. All students enrolled in departmental courses are given printed information on the usefulness of foreign languages in various careers, and individual counseling is available upon request.

Students are strongly encouraged to double major or to major/minor in related areas. The department requires all foreign language majors to demonstrate competence in a second language up to and including the fifth semester in a language sequence. Furthermore, special efforts are made to collect systematic information on reasons for attrition. Students who drop a course or who do not complete a required sequence are sent a self-addressed, stamped postcard requesting them to check their reasons for not continuing in a course sequence.

Finally, the foreign language department at WSU has established an effective recruiting and public relations program consisting of publications, departmental activities, media programming, and advertising. An annual newsletter is sent to alumni, and an attractive and informative brochure is mailed to incoming freshmen, who may request more specific information by self-addressed postcard. The department publishes extensive descriptions of course content, materials, and evaluation procedures; these leaflets are available in a display rack in the departmental office and are routinely sent to all academic advisers. In addition, students are actively recruited through the foreign language career colloquiums mentioned above, and special certificates, awards, and scholarships are given annually to majors and students excelling in foreign language study on all levels. Visibility outside the department is maintained in a number of ways, including three hours of daily radio programming in a foreign language (one hour each in French, German, and Spanish) over the university radio station. Departmental curricular and extracurricular offerings and activities are well advertised in all available media and keep the department constantly visible in the community. Even the doors of the restrooms are used for announcements of coming events such as foreign language films, speakers, theater performances, or other programs.

For further information write

Professor Jean-Charles Seigneuret
Chairman, Department of Foreign Languages and Literatures
Washington State University
Pullman, Washington 99613.

PART TWO: TWO-YEAR COLLEGES

5 | *SUMMARY OF FINDINGS*

Of the 964 two-year institutions on the MLA computerized mailing list, only 181 (18.8%) completed the survey questionnaire. Five institutions (.5%) were no longer in existence, and 22 (2.3%) responded that foreign languages were not—or were no longer—offered. This leaves the total response at 208, or 21.6%. Because of the low response rate and the fact that no efforts were made to randomize the sample, no valid generalizations can be made concerning the situation of foreign languages in two-year institutions. Appendix C presents an analysis of the responding sample so that the findings may be put in perspective.

Enrollment and staffing trends for the period investigated are not encouraging. Although the 433 responding language sections in two-year institutions reported an overall increase in foreign language enrollments of 1,386 students (4.1%), only Spanish, Italian, and the less commonly taught languages showed actual gains in enrollments. Spanish accounted for 75.8% of the growth, Italian for 10.5%, and the less commonly taught languages and general non-language specific courses for 13.7%. If one places the overall enrollments in the context of total institutional growth, only 22 departments (12.1%) were able to attract numbers of students proportionate to institutional growth. The order of popularity of the various languages in the sample investigated is similar to that reported by Kant in 1969.[26] Spanish is by far the most popular language, followed by French, German, Italian, and Russian.

The responding two-year institutions reported a total loss of 38.3 faculty positions (8.2%) for the four-year period investigated. For complete statistics on language enrollments, staffing, and average course loads, see Appendix C. Foreign language requirements, new courses and programs, and testing and evaluation practices are described below.

Only a few of the responding two-year institutions indicated a foreign language requirement for their own programs. Of the 181 respondents, 35 (19.3%) listed a requirement for the A.A. or A.S. degrees in selected disciplines (including law enforcement, bilingual education, social sciences, and humanities). Five departments (2.8%) mentioned that foreign language courses are optional under humanities requirements, and 3 (1.7%) have an obligatory math or foreign language option. Most institutions indicated that their foreign language courses serve prospective transfer students who wish to fulfill a requirement before entering a four-year program. Of those colleges with a foreign language requirement, 19 permit satisfaction of the requirement through placement/proficiency testing, 4 permit elementary courses in several languages, and 1 accepts literature in translation courses and introduction to linguistics and culture.

The 181 respondents from two-year colleges reported a total of 246 new courses introduced between 1972 and 1976. The large majority of these courses consist of traditional introductory or intermediate language courses in languages not previously taught and conversational language tracks or courses (practical German, intensive oral practice, conversational Spanish for bilingual students, French conversation workshop, and so forth) for credit and non-credit. What follows is a selected list of course titles arranged under general headings to indicate areas of course development (excluding traditional four-skills courses). An asterisk indicates that similar courses have been developed in languages other than that specified in the title of a course.

Culture/Civilization/ Literature
(Some of the courses listed were offered as one-credit minicourses.)

    Czech Ethnic Heritage Studies
    The French Heritage in America
   *Introduction to French Culture
    French Art
    France Today: The Country
    France Today: The People
    Contemporary Germany
    Germany 1918–Present
   *The Culture of Mexico
   *Hispanic Culture and Civilization
    Hispanic Life and Institutions
    Hispanic Film
   *Hispanic Short Story
    Social Themes in Latin American Literature
    Children's Literature in Spanish
    Art and Literature in Spanish Golden Age
    Puerto Rican Studies (Civilizacion y literatura de Puerto Rico)
    Literature, Culture, and Civilization of Greater Antilles
   *Survey of Literature
   *Literature in Translation

Career-Related and Special Skills Courses
(While most career-related courses were offered in Spanish, some were available in French, German, Italian, and Portuguese.)

   *German for Travelers
    Intermediate German for Music Majors
   *Italian for Tourists

Portuguese for Nurses
Bilingual Secretarial Training
Introduction to Bilingual/Bicultural Education
*Spanish for Business and Travel
Commercial Spanish
Career Spanish
Spanish for Community Workers
Spanish for the Service Professions
Spanish for Human Services
Spanish for Law Enforcement Personnel
Spanish for Public Service Employees
Spanish Conversation for Health Personnel
Spanish for the Medical Professions
Spanish for Police and Fire Department Personnel
Career Spanish for Hotel Students
Barrio Spanish

Courses Implying Non-Traditional Teaching Approaches
Intensive French
Teaching French to Young Children
*Multilevel Spanish
Spanish on TV
*Study Tour in Mexico
Bilingual Children's Program
Spanish for Native Speakers

General Introduction to Language
Insights into Communication
Languages of Man

Following is a summary of responses indicating the number of two-year colleges offering innovative or non-traditional courses and/or methodological approaches.

Type of Course/Approach	Depts. indicating availability No.	(%)	Comparative percentage of 4-year depts. offering option
Community-oriented courses aimed at special non-matriculated students	81	(44.8)	23
Career-related courses	41	(22.7)	31
Introduction to language/linguistics	34	(18.8)	47
Literature in translation	30	(16.6)	64
Off-campus courses	24	(13.3)	8
Intensive or accelerated courses	23	(12.7)	50
Language courses for native speakers	22	(12.2)	11
Summer programs abroad	20	(11)	18
Contemporary culture (taught in English)	19	(10.5)	24
Contemporary culture (taught in FL)	17	(9.4)	48
Interdisciplinary courses (total)	16	(8.8)	44
Interdisciplinary courses staffed within 1 dept.	3	(1.7)	
Interdisciplinary courses staffed by members of 2 or more depts.	13	(7.2)	
Ethnic studies (taught in English)	14	(7.7)	6

Comparative literature	11 (6.1)	22
Comparative cultures (taught in English)	10 (5.5)	7
Special topics courses, major focus on aspects of language		
or literature	10 (5.5)	38
Academic-year programs abroad	9 (5)	28
Team teaching	8 (4.4)	21
Area studies (taught in English)	7 (3.9)	18
Multilanguage or exploratory courses	5 (2.8)	6
Internships	5 (2.8)	17
Special themes courses, major focus not on language or		
literature	5 (2.8)	16
Immersion courses	3 (17)	
Area studies (taught in FL)	3 (1.7)	14
Translation of specialized materials	2 (1.1)	14
Ethnic studies (taught in FL)	2 (1.1)	7
Comparative cultures (taught in FL)	1 (.6)	6
Courses in which the use of media is a major integrated		
component		
Audio/tape (also language lab)	70 (38.7)	36
Slide/filmstrip	35 (19.3)	24
Film	30 (16.6)	24
Multimedia	27 (14.9)	12
TV	16 (8.8)	7
Computer-assisted instruction	3 (1.7)	4
Radio	1 (.6)	1
Individualized instruction		
One-to-one tutorial or small group	35 (19.3)	22
Self-paced instruction	24 (13.3)	11
Audio/tutorial, independent study	21 (11.6)	10
Programmed instruction	17 (9.4)	6
Minicourses	10 (5.5)	6
Multilevel grouping	1 (.6)	
Contract study	1 (.6)	

Only six departments (3.3%) offer less commonly taught languages, mostly with self-instructional materials.

'Comparison reveals that two-year colleges are clearly more traditional in their offerings and approaches than are four-year institutions. Many two-year language programs are too small to permit much innovation. If one examines the columns indicating the percentage of departments offering various non-traditional options, curricular differences are obvious. Literature in translation (64%), intensive or accelerated courses (50%), contemporary culture taught in a foreign language (48%), introduction to language/linguistics (47%), and interdisciplinary courses (44%) are the five most frequent "innovations" in four-year foreign language departments; community-oriented courses for non-matriculated students (44%), career-related courses (22%), introduction to language/linguistics courses (19%), literature in translation (16%), and off-campus courses (13%) are the five most common non-traditional offerings in two-year departments.

In terms of testing and evaluation practices, of the 181 responding two-year departments, only 34 (18.8%) indicated regular use of systematic placement procedures. Three (1.7%) administer aptitude tests, and 25 (13.8%) regularly give common departmental achievement tests in the various courses taught. Attitude measures were listed by only 3 institutions (1.7%). The tests used by two-year institutions are similar to those administered in four-year colleges.

Departmentally constructed exams are the most common placement and achievement measures, followed by the MLA Cooperative Tests. Very few institutions administer the CLEP and Pimsleur Achievement tests, and the Pimsleur Language Aptitude Battery is used by only a couple of departments. No particular tests for attitude measurement were specified.

6 | *MAJOR PROBLEMS*

Judging from the letters and comments received from two-year institutions, faculty morale is low and a general discontent is apparent among foreign language teachers. The low response rate to the questionnaire study may in itself be an indication of the feeling of futility and lack of support experienced by many educators on that level. Frequently, foreign language teachers in community colleges feel ignored and isolated. They are not part of the secondary scene; nor do they function under the same constraints as their colleagues in four-year institutions. Even professional organizations and journals appear to neglect their special concerns and problems. Apart from an occasional article dealing with specific issues relating to foreign language instruction in two-year institutions, the last intensive intraprofessional efforts to address the problems of the two-year college were made, to my knowledge, in 1972 at the Conference on Foreign Languages in Junior and Community Colleges, held in Illinois.[27] Arthur Cohen, in his ongoing study of the humanities in two-year colleges, has reviewed the available literature and described general characteristics of community college foreign language faculty and curricular patterns.[28]

While four-year and two-year institutions have many problems in common (see chapter ii), foreign language instruction in community colleges faces some particular problems that are less frequently encountered by four-year departments. The most common, described below, are curricular emphasis on technical/vocational education, dependency on foreign language requirements and *de facto* curricular approval by area four-year institutions, restricted offerings (usually limited to service courses on the freshman and sophomore levels), lack of strong departmental structure, extensive use of part-time faculty, little administrative flexibility, open admissions, and a relatively transient (and often part-time) student body.

In many two-year colleges, foreign language study is not considered an essential, integral part of the curriculum. Generally speaking, the curricular emphasis is technical/vocational and career-preparatory, and few institutions give equal emphasis to the humanities or liberal arts. While Cohen, in his 1976 publication, views the state of the humanities in two-year institutions rather optimistically, many foreign language educators apparently see little cause for optimism. Administrators in two-year colleges occasionally consider foreign languages a curricular "frill," inessential to major institutional purposes; in the frank admission of one administrator, foreign language offerings are considered "window dressing." Frequently, the tight structure of vocational programs leaves little time for electives, and uncooperative or uninformed advisers do not direct students into foreign language courses.

Because no two-year foreign language degree exists, the great majority of offerings are of the service variety, geared predominantly toward fulfilling language requirements for prospective transfer students to four-year programs. Enrollments thus appear to be highly dependent on the foreign language requirements of four-year institutions in the area. A number of community colleges reported near collapse of their programs because four-year schools in the vicinity have decreased or abolished requirements.

Four-year institutions also directly and indirectly limit offerings in two-year colleges by awarding (or refusing to award) transfer credit to those who take their courses. Often this practice discourages experimentation and restricts two-year institutions to conventional offerings on the freshman and sophomore levels. Thus, the students with an extensive high school foreign language background often have no meaningful opportunity to continue their study in community colleges.

Another problem is that foreign languages are frequently taught under the auspices of generalist "umbrella" departments (such as humanities, communications, language arts, and so forth), usually chaired by a specialist in a field other than foreign languages, and with primary interests in another discipline. Therefore, foreign languages on the community college level often have no one who represents their interests directly and aggressively and who serves on policy making committees.

Furthermore, a high percentage of foreign language courses on the community college level are taught by part-time temporary faculty. Occasionally, the number of part-time staff members outnumbers those on full-time appointment. Evening programs are at times staffed exclusively by part-time instructors, and even fully employed faculty often teach in two or more unrelated fields. Establishing common objectives and evaluation criteria, ensuring articulation among courses and levels, and providing for program development and continuity thus become difficult tasks, and instructors complain of a serious lack of communication.

Surprisingly, even in this day of oversupply of trained teachers, one still encounters instructors who have no formal training in foreign languages or who lack special preparation (and inclination) for lower-division language teaching. Several administrators mentioned the need for specialized training for teachers in two-year institutions and pointed to a preference for hiring foreign language generalists rather than individuals trained as research-oriented specialists.

Because of the small number of staff available in most two-year foreign language departments, the course schedule is a rigid one; courses are offered in a set sequence and at specific time intervals only (i.e., students can start language study only in the fall and must continue the sequence in winter, or wait a full year before the course is offered again). While four-year colleges are often able to offer courses in spite of very small enrollments, community colleges appear to have less flexibility in waiving minimum enrollment quotas, which are occasionally as high as seventeen students per course. Yet foreign language faculty members believe that courses should be offered even if enrollments do not justify them on a financial basis; after students have made an initial investment of time and money, they have a right to expect continuity.

Finally, the development of strong foreign language programs is limited by the interests of the students. Because of the non-selective admissions policy (and reduced fee structure) of most community colleges, two-year institutions attract a larger range of interests and abilities than do four-year institutions. Many students in community colleges study foreign languages "just for fun" and become easily discouraged when they find out that gaining the expected benefits takes much time, work, and energy. Another limiting factor is that two-year colleges are mostly commuter institutions with a more transient population than one finds in their four-year counterparts. Many students attend classes only part-time and hold full- or part-time employment. This situation makes it difficult to establish departmental cohesion and an esprit de corps among students and faculty through extracurricular activities.

In summary, most of the problems mentioned in this chapter are not new. They are similar to those listed already by Rivers et al. and reviewed by Cohen (see notes 27 and 28, p. 79). Unfortunately, most of these problems are linked to the special purposes and goals of two-year institutions, and no easy solutions are in sight.

7 | FACTORS INFLUENCING ENROLLMENT GROWTH

Time and financial constraints permitted visitation of only four two-year institutions. The schools selected were the City College of San Francisco, Portland Community College-Sylvania Campus (Oregon), San Antonio College (Texas), and Tarrant County Junior College-Northeast Campus (Texas).

All of these institutions are medium to large, publicly financed commuter colleges located in or near major population centers. Three institutions have separate departments of foreign languages, but at Portland Community College foreign languages are taught in the Language Arts Division, which includes English. The usual teaching load in all four institutions is fifteen hours per week. All schools indicated program growth during the four-year period investigated. While Portland Community College and Tarrant County Junior College are limited to regular instruction in the most commonly taught languages, City College of San Francisco and San Antonio College offer a wide variety of languages. For instance, in addition to French, German, and Spanish, City College offers Chinese, Pilipino, Russian, and Swahili.

Of the four schools visited, San Antonio College had the largest program, with a total fall 1976 enrollment of 2,999 students and a full-time-equivalent faculty of 22 for the daytime program. The department provides instruction in classical Greek, Hebrew, Italian, Japanese, Latin, Portuguese, and Russian in addition to the three most commonly taught languages. The phenomenal increase of 1,411 students (89%) recorded between the autumn terms of 1972 and 1976 was predominantly due to growth of the Spanish program (1,146 students) and to the implementation of a successful English as a Second Language program, which grew from 52 students in 1972 to 303 students in 1976. The college is among the very few institutions offering a two-year A.A. degree in translation of scientific and technical materials (Spanish/English). To my knowledge, the only other institution that has such a program is Rose-Hulman Institute of Technology in Indiana. Candidates for the San Antonio program must show some fluency in Spanish before being accepted.

Given the small response rate to the questionnaire and the limited sample of colleges visited, it is difficult to generalize a "recipe for success" that might be of use to other two-year institutions located in different areas and functioning under different constraints. As was the case with four-year colleges, few two-year schools were able to explain their growth solely in terms of curricular changes. External factors such as overall institutional growth, change of ethnic composition of the community and the student body, and an increasing awareness of the usefulness of Spanish (particularly in areas with large Spanish speaking populations, e.g., Texas, California, New York, Arizona, and New Mexico) contributed to an increase in foreign language enrollments. For instance, while San Antonio College has no formal foreign language requirement for its various programs, there is a tacit understanding in many vocational programs that students take at least some Spanish.

Generally speaking, responses to the questionnaire provided little helpful information that can be utilized by institutions with enrollment problems. With few exceptions, departments expressed complaints or attitudes of resignation rather than reporting active efforts to change the situation. Nonetheless, based on the four programs visited, the following factors seem worthy of consideration in efforts to make foreign language study more attractive and more accessible in two-year institutions: emphasis on instructional quality; tracking or adjustment of course content to accommodate a more heterogeneous student body; emphasis on practical conversational language use; career-related courses or courses meeting special community interests; low-credit individual interest electives; and flexible scheduling. These factors are described in detail below.

As in four-year institutions, all two-year department chairpersons credited their instructional staff as the number one factor responsible for success in attracting more students. Chairpersons often named particular individuals for single-handedly increasing enrollments by their excellence in teaching, concern for students' performance, and accessibility to students in need of help. Visitation to the four campuses revealed imaginative teaching and remarkable student fluency.

All chairpersons pointed to the availability and amount of personal contact between faculty and students as factors contributing to success. Many two-year institutions mandate a generous number of office hours per week (e.g., ten hours at Tarrant County Junior College) or require faculty to spend a set number of hours per instructional day on campus (e.g., seven hours at Portland Community College). Judging from the frequent interruptions by students during conversations with faculty members, students take advantage of this open-door policy.

Course modification and tracking systems are other means of attracting students and keeping them in foreign language programs. Because of a non-selective admissions policy in many colleges and a rather heterogeneous student body, some departments have reduced course content to enable a larger number of students to succeed in learning a foreign language. Some institutions offer a two-track system: one covering traditional course content within traditional time periods and usually available for transfer credit to four-year institutions; the other with more limited objectives and a slower pace, usually non-transferable. City College of San Francisco, for instance, has such a system, essentially offering three options: the traditional two-course introductory sequence, which is accepted for credit at state universities; a slowed down version of the same course, which covers in two semesters the material traditionally presented in one; and an introductory "practical" track (emphasis on the spoken language) that is not transferable for university credit.

City College of San Francisco and San Antonio College also have a special track for native Spanish-speaking students. This option is necessitated by the large number of students of Spanish background who want to improve the knowledge of their mother tongue or become literate in it. The Foreign Language Department at the University of Texas at El Paso has also developed such a track because faculty felt that the presence of native Spanish speakers was discouraging students without Hispanic background from majoring in Spanish. Unfortunately, such tracks are not a perfect solution either since those students classified as "Hispanic" often vary considerably in language background and fluency, making accurate placement difficult. In any one class, there may be students with heavy Spanish accents and others, also Spanish-surnamed, who know very little Spanish. One "Hispanic" who had obvious problems with an exercise in class later complained in conversation that "they expect me to know the language just because my grandfather speaks it."

Another trend that is more pronounced in two-year than in four-year institutions is the shift in emphasis from a formal grammatical approach to more practical communication with a focus on conversational abilities. All two-year colleges visited offer low-credit conversation courses on different levels that can be taken independently or simultaneously with traditional four-skills courses. Non-credit or low-credit courses focusing on "survival language" for prospective travelers to a foreign country are also popular. Even though credit for these conversation tracks or courses is often non-transferable to four-year institutions, many students choose them simply to improve or maintain fluency.

Career-related courses also fall into the realm of the practical, conversational category. San Antonio College and Tarrant County Junior College offer instruction to law enforcement and medical personnel on and off campus at the request of community agencies. It is surprising, however, that while many community agencies see the need for language training for their *in-service* personnel, the academic programs preparing prospective employees of those same agencies seldom consider *pre-service* training essential. Although foreign language educators maintain that job-specific language skills can be acquired easily after one has some general background in a language, apparently we have not yet convinced too many colleagues in other fields.

Community colleges, by their nature and purpose, need to be responsive to community needs and interests. Teaching firemen, policemen, doctors, nurses, and other paramedical personnel, social workers, telephone operators, receptionists, bus and taxi drivers, sales personnel, bank tellers, or legal personnel a functional speaking ability in a foreign language falls into this category. Evening courses, providing prospective travelers or business people with insights into the language and culture of a country, literature in translation courses, courses in ethnic cooking—all provide some service to the community and important interaction between a department and the public. In the words of William Samelson of San Antonio College, "You ask us, we teach it—anytime, anywhere." Among other activities, San Antonio College conducts instruction off campus in senior citizens' centers. For those institutions offering career-supportive language training, Samelson also points to the importance of establishing an advisory board consisting of prominent area residents. Not only do these consultants give important input into what should be taught; they also provide valuable contacts for graduating students looking for employment.

While one-hour conversation courses have already been mentioned, other low-credit options are also popular. Students enrolled in career-preparatory programs in community colleges seldom have much time in their schedules for electives. Often the availability of a one- or two-credit course determines whether they can continue their language study. Usually offered under a general title such as "Special Studies" or "Practicum," these courses are similar to minicourses and can be taken for independent study or in small groups. Each term, different topics or skills can be emphasized, permitting students to repeat the courses for credit as often as they wish. Portland Community College, for instance, offers one-hour courses on the second-year level in grammar review (students work through a grammar workbook under the direction of an instructor) and in reading (either literary selections or writings from the popular press), as well as conversation courses on various levels.

Wisely planned and coordinated, such offerings can constitute an intensive program providing up to seven hours of language instruction per week. This instruction, coupled with the availability of a proficiency examination and certificate at the end of two years of instruction, could attract a number of students who would like to acquire fluency in a foreign language for use in their chosen profession.

As mentioned above, two-year departments are often forced into a rigid schedule of course offerings because of staff constraints. In most community colleges, students can begin introductory language study only in the autumn and must continue with the sequence the following term. Portland Community College, however, has devised a scheduling pattern that permits students to start language study during the winter quarter and still complete one year of language study during the same academic year. The student who is not able to commence the sequence of three four-credit courses in the fall may enroll in a more intensive six-credit class during the winter term; the intensive course covers the regular 101 syllabus as well as about half of that for the 102 course. The student can then finish the first year of language study in the spring quarter with another six-hour course.

Since all four institutions visited offer solid programs and have aggressive leadership and excellent faculties, it is difficult to single out one department for special attention. The situation at Tarrant County Junior College, however, is probably more typical than that of the other institutions visited, and I have selected it for a more detailed treatment in the next chapter. Tarrant County Junior College lacks the heavy influx of Hispanic-background peoples that benefited San Antonio College and the cosmopolitan atmosphere that surrounds City College of San Francisco.

For additional information on the four two-year institutions described above write

Professor Jacquelyn W. Green, Chairperson
Foreign Language Department
City College of San Francisco
50 Phelan Ave.
San Francisco, California 94112

Ms. Marcia Marvin, Coordinator of Foreign Languages
Language Arts Division
Portland Community College
12000 S.W. 49th
Portland, Oregon 97219

Dr. William Samelson, Chairperson
Foreign Language Department
San Antonio College
1300 San Pedro Ave.
San Antonio, Texas 78284

Dr. Jane Harper, Chairperson
Department of Foreign Languages
Northeast Campus—Tarrant County Junior College
828 Harwood Road
Hurst, Texas 76053.

8

DESCRIPTION OF SELECTED PROGRAM

Tarrant County Junior College—Northeast Campus

Tarrant County Junior College-Northeast Campus has had considerable success in attracting students to the study of foreign languages. The ten-year-old commuter campus has approximately 7,500 students and is one of three branch campuses in the district, located in a predominantly middle-class suburb of Fort Worth. Compared with some Texas communities, the area has a relatively low proportion of residents of Spanish background. The Northeast Campus attracts many housewives and retired individuals, and the average age of the student body is 27 years.

The foreign language department offers French, German, and Spanish, with four full-time and nine part-time instructors. During the four-year period investigated, foreign language enrollments increased by 65% (231 students), while total institutional growth was about 24%. As in all other programs visited, Spanish showed the largest gains (166 students, or 84%), followed by German (44, or 76%) and French (23, or 23%). Spring 1978 enrollment figures indicated a 13% departmental enrollment growth over spring 1977, while the overall student population showed a decrease.

Tarrant County Junior College has a requirement for the A.A. degree that can be satisfied by eight hours of conventional foreign language study or three hours of mathematics. Looking at the catalogue, the initial impression the outsider gains of the program is that of a rather conventional one, with the usual sequence of introductory and intermediate courses, a one-hour practicum option, and some intermediate-level courses in history, civilization, and culture available in each language. Career-related instruction is available to law enforcement and medical personnel and to students in a bilingual secretarial training program. Upon closer inspection, however, one notices several factors that single out the department as a carefully planned and exceptionally well-coordinated one.

Most important is a clear departmental philosophy that all instructional personnel appear to share and to practice. This philosophy emphasizes mastery of content, rather than time spent in learning, and lessens the threat of failure for many students. The program is not an individualized/self-paced one in the common definition (the four-credit-hour elementary language courses meet regularly for three classroom contact hours per week and require two hours of individual practice in the language laboratory; for the three-credit hour intermediate sequence, laboratory practice is optional). Yet, it has adapted elements of individualization to accommodate a variety of student abilities and interests.

Although the course content is covered in a set progression by all students, most testing is done on an individual basis, outside the classroom, when students feel they have mastered the material. A test bank for self-paced testing is available in the language laboratory. Students are permitted up to four retakes of all written tests until one week before final examinations. The final exam can be repeated only once. Contracts specify the amount of work and the mastery level a student must reach for a desired grade. These grades are renegotiable with individual instructors at mid-term if a student has either underestimated or overestimated his capacity.

Instructors in multisection courses use common departmental tests—a practice deemed important for articulation between courses and levels—because of the part-time staff who might not yet be familiar with program objectives and materials.

Tarrant County Junior College not only proclaims oral communicative goals but actually attempts systematic testing of them in the language laboratory and in frequent individual interviews. In introductory German courses, for instance, about seventy-five percent of the grade is determined by oral work. On the intermediate level, while instruction covers all language skills, students can choose which skill(s) they wish to emphasize in testing. Since much of the testing is done in the language laboratory under the general supervision of laboratory personnel, the elaborate testing program and the retest option do not require inordinate amounts of faculty time.

Especially popular among the course offerings at Tarrant County Junior College are a series of one-hour electives entitled "Practicum." After two semesters of introductory language instruction, students may enroll in these courses alone or concurrently with other intermediate courses. Since practicum courses are offered on various topics, one may earn credit for several of the courses. Some of the options are short stories (several courses), linguistics, conversation (three levels), business correspondence, personal correspondence, and independent student projects. Students may also obtain one-hour practicum credit for tutoring fellow students in need of help. The instructional materials for the practicum courses are often available in learning activities packages that specify objectives, required and optional activities, and evaluation procedures.

In addition to a dedicated faculty and a carefully planned program, Tarrant County Junior College offers excellent instructional facilities. Classrooms are well equipped with access to most types of media, which are used extensively in instruction. The well-organized collection of software (tapes, slides, student-produced video-tapes, filmstrips, language master cards, and games) might be the envy of any foreign language department. Much of the material is "homemade" and coordinated with commercially available materials. French uses Thomas H. Brown, *French: Listening, Speaking, Reading, Writing* (New

York: McGraw-Hill, 1971) for elementary language instruction, heavily supplemented by teacher-constructed materials. Spanish uses the *Zarabanda* film series for four semesters of language study, and German has adopted the Chilton Materials: *Deutsch durch audio-visuelle Methode.*

The language laboratory has been developed into an effective instructional support system. It not only serves the obvious function of providing practice in oral skills but also serves as media library and distribution center and, as already mentioned, as test administration center. The laboratory is open daily from 8:00 a.m. to 10:00 p.m. and is staffed by a full-time day director and a part-time night director, aided by student assistants. The laboratory staff is paid by the library resource center budget. The facilities are used not only by foreign language students but by students and faculty from other departments for listening and tape duplication services.

The foreign language department also has an elaborate public relations, recruiting, and placement program. Brochures and a slide/tape presentation on foreign language programs and offerings can be used in area high schools and community agencies for informational and recruiting purposes. In addition, the department attempts to provide extracurricular activities for students and the community in the form of an annual international film festival. After recruiting new students, the college provides a systematic placement program that utilizes the comprehensive and diagnostic final tests for its regular courses. Resulting student placement is considered quite satisfactory and dependable. In the opinion of the chairwoman, the introductory language program would be even larger than it is now, were it not for the many advanced placements made.

The instructional staff at Tarrant County Junior College is a highly committed one. Refreshingly, they do not just belabor their problems, but actively plan for future curricular modifications. A year-round preparatory program in French and Spanish for children between the ages of five and twelve has been implemented in the summer of 1978. A long-term attitudinal study is under way that should provide valuable insights into relationships between student self-image and interest and achievement in foreign language study. Furthermore, the foreign language staff at Tarrant County Junior College is aware of its changing population and the trend toward an older student body and is thinking of offerings that might appeal to more mature students.

The nicest compliment to the program came from students. Two of the eight students interviewed were enrolled in area four-year institutions but came to Tarrant County Junior College for the purpose of studying a foreign language. (For more details on the program, see Jane Harper, "A Behavioral Learning System in Foreign Languages at Tarrant County Junior College," *Foreign Language Annals*, 8 (1975), 327–34.)

CONCLUSION: SUMMARY AND RECOMMENDATIONS

This study has attempted to find some consensus concerning what areas present major problems in foreign language learning in higher education in the United States. It has also sought factors that have contributed to growth in those departments that have not suffered from the recent national trend of declining enrollments. During the course of the research, similar questions were posed to faculty members, chairpersons, coordinators, administrators, and students on all levels of instruction, as well as to teaching assistants. Usually opinions agreed; occasionally they conflicted. In some departments, the reasons for program success were obvious; in others, those interviewed could not pinpoint specific program modifications but attributed growth mostly to favorable external conditions. Some departments considered themselves "innovative"; others took pride in being "solidly traditional."

Essentially, the inquiries found little that had not been discussed already in either professional publications or conferences. Many of the problems confronting undergraduate foreign language instruction have been recognized, and possible solutions have been proposed. What is disconcerting is that educators keep listing the problems but do not appear to listen to, or act on, the recommendations—at least, there is no means of knowing who implements what suggestions.

This study is not an all-inclusive overview of "successful" curricular practices or enrollment trends. The findings are based on a small, non-randomized sample, including only those departments that responded to the request for information. In interpreting the findings pertaining to the four-year institutions, the reader is reminded that 400 (58%) of the questionnaire responses came from private institutions and 439 (63%) of the responding departments were located in institutions with fewer than 5,000 students.

The numerical findings of the questionnaire study (four-year institutions) can be easily summarized:

- Enrollments have continued their general downward trend in all commonly taught languages except Spanish.
- Since 1972, the proportion of students enrolled in higher education who studied a foreign language has declined.
- Fewer students were majoring in foreign languages in 1976 than in 1972 (with the exception of Italian and Russian).
- A considerable number of foreign language teachers have lost their positions because of program reductions.
- Judging by the loss of teaching assistantships, graduate programs also appear to have suffered a decline.
- A large number of institutions report eliminating or decreasing foreign language requirements in the last decade.
- In the area of assessment and evaluation, measurement of aptitude and attitude is practically nonexistent. Systematic measurement of achievement/proficiency is mentioned by only 190 departments (27%)—a disconcertingly low number for this supposed age of emphasis on accountability, educational outcomes, and learning rather than teaching.

Although the numerical findings of the questionnaire study from two-year colleges are not quite so bleak as those from four-year institutions, Spanish and Italian are the only major languages reporting enrollment increases.

The most commonly listed factors that, in the opinion of responding department chairpersons, contributed to the decline in enrollments were:

- elimination or reduction of foreign language requirements;
- change in student attitudes toward foreign language study and decreasing quality of preparation in English, affecting the ability to master a foreign language;
- reduction of faculty and program offerings because of budget cuts;
- lack of support by administrators or faculties in other disciplines, which manifests itself in indifferent advising of students (few foreign language departments appear to have established any rapport with colleagues or systematic means of communication with those responsible for general academic advising);
- reduction in quantity and quality of high school programs; and
- proliferation of new academic majors and the offering of languages not previously taught.

In addition to these problems, respondents from two-year colleges mentioned

- the curricular emphasis on technical/vocational education;
- dependency on four-year institutions for curricular approval;
- offerings limited to service courses on the freshmen and sophomore levels;
- extensive use of part-time faculty;
- little administrative flexibility;
- a short-term, transient student body.

While these problems are certainly real and undoubtedly affect enrollments, they place the blame on factors that are, to a large extent, outside the direct control of the profession. Other problems that became evident during on-site visitations and discussions with many educators and other individuals concerned with foreign language instruction are:

- the lack of articulation and communication between secondary and postsecondary instruction (little systematic effort is made to establish continuity of instruction from one level to the next, and there are few common goals between secondary and college foreign language programs, except as they are implied in conventional textbooks that "cover" the grammar in two years of high school versus two semesters on the college level);
- the lack of defined competencies a student can expect to gain after specific periods of study;
- the unrealistic expectation implied (but seldom realized) by existing program structures and materials that a student can "master" a foreign language in two to four semesters of study;
- the unrealistic content load of many introductory-level programs, permitting only the exceptional student (in ability and motivation) a chance to succeed and discouraging many students from continuing language study;
- the need for revising the structure and content of the foreign language requirement to make it indeed the broad humanistic experience we claim it can be, rather than the grammatical obstacle course and academic survival test that it too often resembles at present;
- the divisiveness between those foreign language educators with a major interest in language teaching and those who specialize in literary studies (while the former group blames the latter for being "out of touch," elitist, and unrealistic, the latter blames the former for "watering down courses," lowering standards, adulterating the discipline by introducing content in areas for which we lack specialization, and innovating for the sake of innovation);
- the problems in obtaining a fair share of available public and private monies to conduct research into second-language learning and to develop and implement programs and courses known to be effective but too expensive for the average institution.

Areas of concern expressed by students focused on:

- the need for non-literary options in third- and fourth-year courses for those without major interest in a chronological study of authors, periods, or genres (this need was expressed by foreign language majors and non-majors alike);
- the need for more civilization and culture courses on all levels;
- the need for more emphasis on contemporary topics and works in literary studies;
- the need for courses dealing with the literature, civilizations, and cultures of those countries where the target language is spoken, but which are generally neglected in traditional academic offerings (e.g., courses focusing on Latin America rather than Spain; on French speaking West Africa, Canada, or the Caribbean, rather than France; on the DDR, Austria, and Switzerland, rather than Germany before 1945 and the Federal Republic since);
- the lack of transition between highly structured and carefully controlled (in terms of linguistic difficulty) language study during the first two years, followed by the sudden confrontation with the literary masterworks of a culture, written in an idiom appreciably different in style, vocabulary, and register than the materials the student has encountered previously (almost unanimously, advanced

students expressed the need for more language skills courses, especially courses providing practice in writing and translation);
- the need for conducting language and literature courses in the target language. (In the words of one student, "the [target] language is used like some abstract body of material. Whenever the teacher wants to express a personal idea, he resorts to English.")

None of the curricular modifications or methodological approaches reported as successful in attracting and holding student enrollments—be they non-traditional options courses, intensive instruction, study abroad, extracurricular offerings, internships, avid public relations, or any other factor mentioned in the chapters of this report—should be considered an "instant" solution to the problems of a department. Probably none of the modifications are transferable in toto, at least without extensive modifications. Each department has its own special setting and constraints that must be taken into account before attempting to make program changes. Only after a department has made a clear assessment of its purpose(s), function(s), location, institutional setting, student body, number and specialties of available staff, administrative support, and general resources should it determine necessary and possible program modifications. Further, each department should establish definite priorities for what it wants to accomplish. Does it want to achieve a high level of competence by a few? Give general insights and provide successful learning experiences to many? Provide training in specific skills? All of these aims are valid, but few departments can accomplish them well concurrently.

What, then, are some general characteristics of the programs visited that might have increased enrollments in foreign languages? While each program is unique in setting as well as approach, all have some traits that might well be examined by those departments evaluating their own programs: 1) strong leadership by the chairperson; 2) an open, cooperative, and active faculty; 3) the ability to instill in students a feeling of confidence that foreign language learning is a possible, rewarding, and worthwhile task; and 4) an awareness that public relations—and all it entails—with the college community and the general public is an important element in the success of a department.

While individual readers will be able to generalize for themselves those program modifications described in chapters iii and vii that might be investigated within their own departments, the following directions should be explored by the profession in general, together with agencies interested in foreign language instruction in the United States and abroad:

Articulation and Communication between Secondary and Postsecondary Instruction. The majority of students who eventually major in a foreign language begin their study in high school. In research conducted by Wilga Rivers, only 4% of the French majors had started the study of French on the college level.[29] Jean Carduner believes that, generally speaking, four years of high school foreign language study are superior to two years at a university and that the best students are usually those who have begun their studies on the secondary level.[30] Carroll's findings of a high positive correlation between length of study and achievement support the importance of an early start for those wanting to specialize in a foreign language.[31]

Yet, communication and articulation between the secondary and postsecondary levels are among the most sorely neglected areas in the profession. While the increasing public relations and recruiting efforts of colleges toward secondary schools are laudable—and surely have some motivational impact— an annual foreign language festival or an occasional recruiting speech by a faculty member is not enough. What is most needed is active communication by educators from all three levels—secondary, community college, and four-year institutions. They must sit down together and exchange information on program objectives, goals, materials, and methods and establish some common guidelines and evaluation criteria for those students who eventually continue foreign language study at an advanced level.

Few secondary teachers have any knowledge of the type of placement tests and procedures utilized in area postsecondary institutions. Yet, for effective articulation, placement instruments should be developed jointly by secondary and postsecondary foreign language programs. Where this is not possible, post-secondary departments should at least supply area foreign language teachers with a sample of the placement test used and inform them of minimal entry criteria for each level.

To reduce the time wasted by students who have studied a foreign language in high school but cannot proceed to the next level in the college sequence— either because of a lack of confidence or because of unsatisfactory performance on a placement test—more postsecondary institutions could provide an intensive review course similar to that offered at the University of Texas at Arlington.[32] Such a course prepares students for the transition between secondary foreign language study and more advanced courses on the college level by providing an introduction to the materials used in the sequence and a quick intensive grammar and vocabulary review.

Some institutions (e.g., the University of Arkansas, Ohio State University, and the University of Oklahoma) avoid the placement dilemma and encourage students with a high school background to continue foreign language study in college by permitting them to enroll in courses above the first introductory term without placement testing. If a student passes such a course at a specified grade (usually B or C), he or she will automatically receive credit for the preceding courses in the sequence, essentially receiving college credit for prior high school study.

Coordination and Articulation among Lower-Division College Courses. Coordination involves developing common goals and measures of achievement in introductory and intermediate multisection courses and in course assignments shared by several faculty members. The discrepancy of content, requirements, and expected achievement in sections of a course taught by different faculty members can be astounding. If the course is one in a required sequence, this discrepancy can have tragic consequences for the student who does not receive adequate preparation for the next course. Department heads should insist on joint development and coordination of multisection courses and courses that rotate among faculty. Each department should keep a file of detailed syllabi and copies of all tests. These syllabi can be modified as often as necessary, but all instructional personnel involved should help make the modifications. It is especially important that lower-division courses providing the basic foundations of a language establish realistic objectives and a content load that can be covered by all instructors and mastered by a majority of students enrolled in the course.

Expansion of Course Options for Foreign Language Majors. Since the traditional foreign language major with an exclusive concentration in literature no longer meets the needs and interests of many students, other major options or concentrations emphasizing areas such as culture/civilization, language/translation, and area studies should be made available. Such concentrations would be particularly useful to students planning a double major in a foreign language and a related discipline.

Developing Foreign Language Proficiency as an Ancillary Skill. A major challenge for the profession is to develop viable and intellectually defensible options to attract generalist students and those majoring in other disciplines. Such students should continue their language study until they actually gain some mastery of the foreign language and understanding of the culture. Regardless of the extent of innovation or diversification, however, it would be unrealistic to expect that we will be able to hold a large number of those who now leave us after one, two, or three semesters of study. The nature and constraints of second-language learning will always appeal to a relatively small group. But surely a substantial number of prospective political, social, or natural scientists, businessmen, physicians, lawyers, or artists would continue foreign language study after a basic introduction if they were offered courses that they felt would fill a particular need and would lead toward some fluency and familiarity with a particular culture.

It would not be feasible for every institution to develop an extensive battery of career-related courses in order to attract the few students who might be interested in such options. The need for individuals with career-specific language training is rather small. Apart from a few specialized programs, universities should focus on giving students a general foundation in language, civilization, and culture. Any student who has acquired such basic fluency and knowledge can easily learn career-specific vocabulary or language skill(s) on the job or in specialized training programs conducted by business or government agencies. The major need is for professionals in all fields with a *general fluency* in at least one foreign language. Specialized career-oriented foreign language courses for students without a general basic foundation in a language are emergency, stopgap measures. While valid (and often necessary) as a community service (e.g., Spanish for firemen, police, and health officials), the value of such courses is limited for the general curriculum.

Developing advanced non-traditional options for the non-specialist foreign language student and making the study of foreign languages a viable adjunct field for students of other disciplines are concerns that might best be explored by the professional organizations. In addition to sponsoring regional or national conferences or workshops on the development of non-traditional options at the advanced (third- and fourth-year) undergraduate level, such organizations could establish a "bank" or "banks" for syllabi, course or program descriptions, and bibliographies for special non-traditional options courses. These banks would serve as a source of stimulation and information to departments and individual faculty members interested in implementing similar courses. Course development is a time- and energy-consuming task; the proposed information bank(s) could prevent duplication of efforts and mistakes. Such a program should be sponsored by a national professional organization, such as ACTFL or the MLA, in order to provide information on new developments in all languages. To make the information collected easily available, and to provide recognition to those professionals who cooperate and share their work, ideas, and experiences, these course descriptions should be in the form of a publication, compiled annually for perusal by interested educators.

Development of Proficiency Certification Procedures. Foreign language educators need to develop nationally recognized tests for at least two levels of proficiency. Each language should establish an active commission to establish realistic minimal competencies in language skills and cultural knowledge for intermediate and advanced undergraduate levels and to develop valid testing instruments and procedures to measure these competencies. While testing could remain optional for individual students, those passing the test could receive a certificate of proficiency. The certificates would have to achieve national and international recognition in order to serve prospective employers, college administrators, and so forth as indicators of an applicant's level of proficiency. Tests could be patterned after those already used in the United States and abroad for large-scale certification of language competence in ESL, French, German, and Spanish. (Such proficiency examinations are now administered by the Educational Testing Service, Cambridge University, the Alliance Française, and the Goethe Institute. In addition, the Deutscher Volkshochschulverband [German Association for Continuing Education], in cooperation with the Goethe Institute and other European educational agencies, has developed a series of basic proficiency tests in all commonly taught languages, and the Council of Europe is working on the development of minimal competence tests in foreign languages.)

There is indeed a pronounced career-orientation among today's college youth. Students and employers alike look favorably on programs that document mastery of certain knowledge and useful skills rather than documenting preparation in the form of academic credits only. (College transcripts are practically meaningless as indicators of proficiency.) Two-year institutions, in particular, would benefit by offering study leading to a certificate of intermediate language proficiency. Community college trained law enforcement, paramedical, secretarial, clerical, or technical personnel who could document fluency in a foreign language (particularly Spanish) would surely have an edge over other applicants in the employment market. Four intensive terms, similar to those available at Portland Community College, could well prepare an interested student for such certification.

Development of Internships or Community Involvement Programs. Internships are predominantly aimed at foreign language majors or at advanced language students who study a language to be used as a supportive skill in another profession. As such, internships cannot be designed as mass programs and usually do not contribute heavily to enrollments. The concept is a popular one, however, mentioned by several institutions, and should be explored by the profession. Especially in large metropolitan areas it should not be too difficult to establish contacts with embassies, consulates, social agencies, travel bureaus, hotels, or other tourist services that would be willing to provide opportunities for students to use their language proficiency in real-life settings. Efforts should also be made on an international basis to establish internships in foreign business, industry, and social and cultural institutions so that students can gain experience in their major field of interest while immersed in another language and culture.

Community involvement activities, similar to those offered by the University of Southern California, can also benefit the foreign language program. Even in non-metropolitan areas without large ethnic minorities, college foreign language students could teach minicourses on the heritage of a particular people or on selected aspects of a culture or civilization to secondary students. Such minicourses, which could be a component of undergraduate culture and civilization courses, would provide a challenging and worthwhile experience for both college and high school students. Teaching short-term foreign language courses to children in elementary schools does not require an urban setting or a large bilingual population. With some thought, surely more possibilities will present themselves for community involvement and activities that utilize a student's linguistic or cultural knowledge, set the stage for close interaction between a foreign language department and the community, and provide challenging and valuable learning experiences for our students.

Foreign Language Degree Requirements. The topic that came up most frequently in discussions with university administrators was the foreign language requirement. I propose the establishment of a commission to investigate degree requirements nationally, to collect and present evidence for or against the validity of a foreign language requirement on the postsecondary level, to make an authoritative statement about requirements, and to propose practical guidelines for institutions that are reevaluating their programs. Such a commission should include representatives from all commonly taught languages as well as specialists from other fields concerned with general education. Let me state for the record that I am not an unqualified proponent of requirements—foreign language or other. The motivation for advocating a foreign language requirement must come not from the need to preserve teaching positions but from the conviction that a society, for its own survival and propagation, needs to share a base of common insights, skills, and values. To justify foreign languages as a general requirement, we must determine just what our discipline can offer that contributes uniquely to the development of such common insights, skills, and values; and we need to reevaluate our offerings in terms of these findings.[33]

Staff Development. Individual institutions or national organizations should sponsor a series of practical regional workshops to provide further training for those who staff foreign language departments. With the help of extramural funding, such workshops could enlist the assistance of a panel of recognized experts and practitioners in various areas and could partially absorb the cost of participation by interested colleges or universities. The following areas should receive priority: program development, the training of teaching assistants, and coordination and supervision of lower-division foreign language instruction; intensive foreign language instruction or immersion programs; advising and career counseling; interdisciplinary programs; articulation between secondary and postsecondary instruction to establish common goals and evaluation measures; workshops addressing special program needs on the two-year college level.

Study Abroad. The National Endowment for the Humanities and other agencies concerned with the lack of second-language ability of Americans could encourage the study of foreign languages by providing—or contributing to—support for study abroad. Study abroad is the quickest and most effective means of acquiring proficiency in another language, especially when the foundations for such study are laid before the students' sojourn abroad. Yet, nationally, little if anything is done to encourage and facilitate such study. Qualified undergraduate students in all fields could receive support in the forms of scholarships, stipends, and low-interest or interest-free loans, or in large-scale exchange arrangements. Such support should also be available for graduate students and teaching staff on a much larger scale than now exists. Since bilingualism and biculturalism essentially benefit two countries, American and foreign agencies concerned with intercultural communication and understanding should cooperate in exchange programs supporting and facilitating large-scale study abroad.

Consortium Approaches. The NEH and other funding agencies should support establishment of regional consortia for the development of special programs such as intensive language instruction, interdisciplinary programs, area studies, and career-related instruction. Most mid-sized and smaller institutions have neither the staff nor the necessary enrollment to make special instructional options feasible. If colleges could be encouraged to pool their resources and students, quality programs could be developed to serve a larger constituency by rotating from institution to institution, thereby avoiding expensive (and frequently unqualified) duplication of efforts.

Consultancies. A panel of consultants should be made available to provide interested departments with some expertise and guidance in planning, developing, and implementing program revisions. In order not to discourage smaller, less endowed institutions, the only requirement for obtaining consultant services should be an extensive internal program evaluation by a department and the expressed wish to move in specific directions. Agencies that currently sponsor such consultant services should work closely with one another and should seek counsel from related professional organizations such as ACTFL, the MLA, and national organizations serving teachers of specific languages and language groups.

Establishment of a Foreign Language Research Fund. Finally, a special fund should be established to support research in second-language learning and in factors affecting second-language learning. This fund should be administered under a national organization concerned with foreign language study and should be controlled by a panel of recognized scholars and researchers in the field.

In conclusion, while recognizing problem areas is relatively easy, searching for possible solutions can be an overwhelming task, especially when one attempts to consider the constraints of the foreign language discipline and of American higher education. The danger is to be carried away by utopian dreaming and recommendations that are neither practical nor feasible in an American setting. The directions suggested above are both realistic and feasible in financial and other terms, however.

Solutions to the problems facing the foreign language profession will not come exclusively from some external agency—some knight in shining armor who can rescue a discipline in distress. Neither can these problems be solved solely by an infusion of funds (though such an injection would certainly help). Essentially, solutions lie in the combined efforts of each individual department, each local, state, regional, and national organization concerned with foreign language instruction—all depending on the efforts of the individual members.

Unfortunately, there is no one organization that represents, guides, informs, and lobbies for all languages and all levels of instruction and that is recognized by all foreign language educators, government agencies, or the general public as spokesman for our cause and our concerns. To have any impact nationally, the numerical strength and support of all individuals concerned with foreign language education must be unified in a *single* organization. This does not necessitate the creation of a new organization. Rather, to repeat the plea made by David P. Benseler at a 1977 ADFL Seminar, all existing organizations must affiliate under one strong umbrella organization that will represent the general needs and interests of *all* foreign language educators.[34]

At present there appears to be increasing awareness of the need for foreign language study and the value of bilingualism in America, as well as an interest in improving foreign language instruction and in making it accessible to a larger segment of the population. The establishment of the President's Commission on Foreign Language and International Studies is a first effort by our national government to honor the commitment made in the Helsinki Agreement, signed in 1975, "to encourage the study of foreign languages and civilizations as an important means of expanding communication among peoples" and "to stimulate . . . the further development and improvement of foreign language teaching." The popular press is taking an increased interest in the problems of the foreign language profession.[35] The "Report on Teaching: 5" in *Change* (January 1978) calls attention to selected innovative programs. The 1977 MLA survey of foreign language enrollments in American colleges and universities shows a slow-down in the decline of foreign language study since 1974. Furthermore, discussions of reinstituting or increasing the foreign language requirement at a number of institutions nationwide, the "back to basics" movement decrying the declining competence in English of college freshmen, the increasing number of grant applications dealing with foreign language study submitted to and funded by public and private foundations—all support our cause and give reason for guarded optimism that foreign language study will regain an important and respected place in American education. Let us use this positive climate to assess ourselves, our purposes, and our programs and move in directions that will not repeat the mistakes of the past.

NOTES AND REFERENCES

[1] Maria P. Alter, *A Modern Case for German* (Philadelphia: American Association of Teachers of German, 1970). See also "A Modern Case for Foreign Languages," *Modern Language Journal*, 60 (1976), 155–59.

[2] James W. Dodge, *The Case for Foreign-Language Study: A Collection of Readings* (Middlebury, Vt.: Northeast Conference, 1971); Frank M. Grittner, "Why Should Americans Study a Foreign Language?" in *Teaching Foreign Languages*, 2nd ed. (New York: Harper, 1977), pp. 22–45; Lucille J. Honig and Richard I. Brod, *Foreign Languages and Careers* (New York: MLA, 1974); Gilbert A. Jarvis, "We Think We Are Evening in Paris, but We're Really *Chanel*," *Foreign Language Annals*, 8 (1975), 104–10; John H. Lawson, "Should Foreign Language Be Eliminated from the Curriculum?" in Lorraine A. Strasheim, ed., *Foreign Language in a New Apprenticeship for Living* (Bloomington: Indiana Univ., 1971), pp. 10–12.

[3] Richard I. Brod, "Foreign Language Enrollments in United States Colleges—Fall 1974," *Modern Language Journal*, 60 (1976), 168–71, and Scott E. Morrison, "Foreign Language Enrollments in U.S. Colleges and Universities—Fall 1977," *ADFL Bulletin*, 10, No. 1 (1978), 13–18.

[4] *Time*, 9 Jan. 1978, p. 57.

[5] Walter F. W. Lohnes and Valters Nollendorfs, eds., *German Studies in the United States: Assessment and Outlook* (Madison: Univ. of Wisconsin Press, 1976).

[6] Kathryn Buck, "Report on the 1974-75 Survey of Non-Traditional Curricula," *ADFL Bulletin*, 7, No. 1 (1975), 12–16.

[7] Maurice W. Conner has described several such interdisciplinary efforts in his chapter "New Curricular Connections," in June K. Phillips, ed., *The Language Connection: From the Classroom to the World*, ACTFL Foreign Language Education Series, No. 9 (Skokie, Ill.: National Textbook Co., 1977), pp. 95–121.

[8] See program description, "Languages and the International Business Connection," in *Change*, 10, No. 1 (1978), 48–49.

[9] Sue Huseman Moretto, "Adapting Foreign Language Programs to Modern Language Needs," *AATF National Bulletin*, 2, No. 4 (1977), 9–12.

[10] John B. Carroll, "Foreign Language Proficiency Levels Attained by Language Majors near Graduation from College," *Foreign Language Annals*, 1 (1967), 131–51.

[11] Letter from Beverly Galyean, Confluent Education Development and Research Center, Santa Barbara, Calif., undated.

[12] For a more detailed description of confluent education see George I. Brown, Mark Phillips, and Stewart Shapiro, *Getting It All Together: Confluent Education* (Bloomington, Ind.: The Phi Delta Kappa Educational Foundation, 1976).

[13] Beverly Colleene Galyean, "The Effects of a Confluent Language Curriculum on the Oral and Written Communication Skills, and Various Aspects of Personal and Interpersonal Growth of a College French Level One Class," Diss. Univ. of California, Santa Barbara, 1977.

[14] Letter from Rivka Dori, Hebrew Union College, 3 June 1977.

[15] Letter from Beverly Galyean, 31 Aug. 1977.

[16] Clay Benjamin Christensen, "Affective Learning Activities (ALA)," *Foreign Language Annals*, 8 (1975), 211–19; and "Achieving Language Competence with Affective Learning Activities," *Foreign Language Annals*, 10 (1977), 157–67.

[17] Virginia Wilson and Beverly Wattenmaker, *Real Communication in Foreign Language* (Upper Jay, N.Y.: The Adirondack Mountain Humanistic Education Center, 1973).

[18] For a more detailed description see Joseph W. Zdenek, "Mini-Courses—A Small Department Changes Its Curriculum to Survive," *Modern Language Journal*, 60 (1976), 468–69. Robert C. Lafayette has described a range of minicourses in his chapter "The Minicourse: A Viable Curricular Alternative," in Gilbert A. Jarvis, ed., *An Integrative Approach to Foreign Language Teaching: Choosing among the Options*, ACTFL Foreign Language Education Series, No. 8, (Skokie, Ill.: National Textbook Co., 1976), pp. 81–127.

[19] For more information contact David Curland, University of Oregon, Department of Romance Languages, Eugene, Oregon.

[20] For more information contact Christian Stehr, Department of Foreign Languages and Literatures, Oregon State University, Corvallis, Oregon.

[21] For a more detailed description see Cecilia C. Baumann, "Internationalizing the Student Body: Pomona College's Oldenborg Center," *ADFL Bulletin*, 8, No. 2 (1976), 45–49.

[22] Barbara S. Gardner, *Building Educational Bridges between Practically Everybody* (Joint Educational Project, Univ. of Southern California, 1977), p. 6.

[23] For more information see Kathleen G. Boykin, "Strategies for Visibility and Recruitment for College and University Language Departments," in Renate A. Schulz, ed., *Personalizing Foreign Language Instruction: Learning Styles and Teaching Options* (Skokie, Ill.: National Textbook Co., 1977), pp. 142–48.

[24] Letter from W. L. Nahrgang, North Texas State University, Denton, Texas, 5 Dec. 1977.

[25] For program descriptions see *Time*, 16 Aug. 1976, p. 56; *New York Times Educational Supplement* (8 Jan. 1978), p. 3; Stan Luxenberg, "All the Class a Stage," *Change*, 10, No. 1 (1978), 33–35.

[26] J. G. Kant, "Foreign Language Registrations in Institutions of Higher Education, Fall 1968," *Foreign Language Annals*, 3 (1969), 247–304.

[27] Wilga M. Rivers, et al., *Changing Patterns in Foreign Language*. Report of the Illinois Conference on Foreign Languages in Junior and Community Colleges, Champaign, 1972 (Rowley, Mass.: Newbury House, 1972).

[28] Arthur M. Cohen, "Foreign Languages in Two-Year Colleges: Curriculum and Instruction," *ADFL Bulletin*, 7, No. 3 (1976), 22–27; Arthur M. Cohen, Florence B. Brawer, and Victor Cruz-Cardona, "The Humanities and Foreign Languages in Community and Junior Colleges," *ADFL Bulletin*, 8, No. 3 (1977), 15–20; and Arthur M. Cohen, "Foreign Languages in the Community College," *ADFL Bulletin*, 9, No. 3 (1978), 7–10.

[29] *Journées d'études sur la diffusion de la langue française aux Etats-Unis* (Paris: Association Linguistique Franco-Européenne, 1974), p. 42.

[30] *Journées d'études*, p. 42.

[31] Carroll, pp. 131–51.

[32] Duane V. Keilstrup, "The Texas Experiment in Coordinating High School and College Language Programs," *ADFL Bulletin*, 6, No. 2 (1974), 45–46.

[33] For a more detailed proposal see Renate A. Schulz, "Back to Basics in the Foreign Language Classroom?" *Foreign Language Annals*, 11 (1978), 647–55.

[34] David P. Benseler, "The Foreign Language Teacher and Professional Associations: Thoughts from the Grave." Paper presented at the Association of Departments of Foreign Languages Seminar East, Philadelphia, June 1977.

[35] For examples see *Newsweek*, 5 Dec. 1977, p. 56; *Time*, 9 Jan. 1978, p. 57.

APPENDIX A

Questionnaire

STATE UNIVERSITY COLLEGE AT BUFFALO

1300 ELMWOOD AVENUE   BUFFALO, NEW YORK 14222

Foreign Language Department   Telephone (716) 862-4126, -5414

February, 1977

Dear Foreign Language Department Head:

Concerned with declining student enrollments in foreign languages, the Division of Education Programs of the National Endowment for the Humanities has funded a study of successful undergraduate foreign language programs. I need your help in order to identify those factors which may contribute to success in attracting students to the study of foreign languages.

While I realize that program growth is but one indicator of success, because of time constraints success has been defined provisionally in terms of enrollment only. Hopefully, the results of this project will permit some generalizations of models, patterns, and approaches to foreign language instruction on the college level which can be reproduced or adapted by other institutions to improve instruction and make foreign language learning more attractive to a larger number of students.

I would be very grateful to you if you could complete the attached questionnaire and return it in the enclosed pre-paid envelope by **March 30, 1977.** From the responding departments a sample of twenty promising programs will be selected for in-depth study. **Please complete the questionnaire even if your departmental enrollment figures have declined over the past five years.** Your responses to the questions will give important insights into overall curricular practices.

You have in advance my sincere thanks, and those of N.E.H., for participating in this study and for taking time away from your busy schedule to complete the questionnaire.

Sincerely,

Renate A. Schulz
Project Director

**SURVEY OF SUCCESSFUL UNDERGRADUATE FOREIGN LANGUAGE PROGRAMS
IN U. S. INSTITUTIONS OF HIGHER EDUCATION
FEBRUARY 1977**

National Endowment for the Humanities, Grant No. EH-27125-77-67

Please answer the following items:

Responding Department: _____

Institution: _____

Address:_____

Name of Chairperson: _____

Contact person for further inquiries (if other than Chairperson):_____

1. What is the highest degree your department offers?

   ☐ B.A./B.S.   ☐ M.A.   ☐ Ph.D. or equivalent   ☐ Other (please specify) _____

2. Number of students enrolled in ALL undergraduate courses taught in your department:

	a) Fall 1972	b) Fall 1974	c) Fall 1976
French	_____	_____	_____
German	_____	_____	_____
Italian	_____	_____	_____
Latin	_____	_____	_____
Russian	_____	_____	_____
Spanish	_____	_____	_____
Other (specify)	_____	_____	_____
Other (specify)	_____	_____	_____
Other (specify)	_____	_____	_____
Total departmental enrollment	_____	_____	_____

3. Number of graduating majors (B.A. and B.S.) in your department (count dual majors twice):

	a) 1971/72	b) 1973/74	c) 1975/76
French	_____	_____	_____
German	_____	_____	_____
Italian	_____	_____	_____
Latin	_____	_____	_____
Russian	_____	_____	_____
Spanish	_____	_____	_____
Other (specify)	_____	_____	_____
Other (specify)	_____	_____	_____

4. Total full-time undergraduate enrollment at your institution:

   a) Fall 1972 _____   b) Fall 1974 _____   c) Fall 1976 _____

1

5. Total number of faculty positions in your department (convert part-time teaching assignments to full-time):

   a) Fall 1972 _____ b) Fall 1974 _____ c) Fall 1976 _____

6. Number of T.A.s in your department:

   a) Fall 1972 _____ b) Fall 1974 _____ c) Fall 1976 _____

7. Average course load per semester/quarter for each full-time instructor:

   Number of courses taught per semester/quarter _____ (Circle appropriate unit.)

   Number of credit hours taught per semester/quarter _____ (Circle appropriate unit.)

8. Does your institution have a language requirement?

   Entrance requirement
   - ☐ No
   - ☐ Yes (specify number of years of high school study.)
     _____ years

   Undergraduate degree requirement
   - ☐ No
   - ☐ Yes (Specify number of sem./qtr. hrs.)
     _____sem. qtr. hrs. (Circle appropriate unit)

   Proficiency requirement
   - ☐ No
   - ☐ Yes (Specify how it may be satisfied.)
     _____

9. What students are affected by language requirements?
   - ☐ all students
   - ☐ B.S. degree students
     Percentage of institutional enrollment in B.S. Program: _____
   - ☐ B.A. degree students
     Percentage of institutional enrollment in B.A. program: _____
   - ☐ other (please specify departments, colleges, or divisions)

10. If you have a foreign language requirement, what options do students have in fulfilling it? (Check all that apply.)
    - ☐ Placement/Proficiency examination
    - ☐ Conventional elementary and intermediate language courses in one foreign language
    - ☐ Conventional language courses in more than one foreign language (e.g., 2 semesters of elementary German and 2 semesters of elementary French)
    - ☐ Special options courses to emphasize certain skills (e.g., parallel multiple tracking in reading, conversation, translation, etc.)
    - ☐ Courses about language, civilization, or culture taught predominantly in English
    - ☐ Literature in translation
    - ☐ Combination of above

2

☐ Other (please specify) _____

_____

_____

_____

11. Has the foreign language requirement at your institution been modified since Fall 1968?

    ☐ No

    ☐ Yes. (check whether requirements have been modified before or since 1972):

        ☐ Before 1972

        ☐ Since 1972

    Please explain changes in requirement and how they have affected enrollments:

_____

_____

_____

_____

_____

12. Please list all NEW courses or programs instituted in your department since fall 1972 which are still offered REGULARLY. (Attach additional sheet, if necessary.)

Course Level (Put 1 for elementary, 2 for intermediate, and 3 for upper level courses.)	Course Title	No. of sem./qtr. credit hours	Enrollment when last offered	Applicable toward requirement	
				Yes	No
_____	_____	_____	_____	☐	☐
_____	_____	_____	_____	☐	☐
_____	_____	_____	_____	☐	☐
_____	_____	_____	_____	☐	☐
_____	_____	_____	_____	☐	☐
_____	_____	_____	_____	☐	☐
_____	_____	_____	_____	☐	☐
_____	_____	_____	_____	☐	☐
_____	_____	_____	_____	☐	☐
_____	_____	_____	_____	☐	☐

13. Please list the 5 courses beyond the elementary level taught in your department which draw the largest student enrollment.

Course Level	Course Title	Sem./qtr. hrs.	Approximate enrollment	Applicable toward requirement	
				Yes	No
_____	_____	_____	_____	☐	☐
_____	_____	_____	_____	☐	☐
_____	_____	_____	_____	☐	☐
_____	_____	_____	_____	☐	☐
_____	_____	_____	_____	☐	☐

14. Please check all undergraduate options, courses, or methodological approaches your department offers and indicate the level(s) at which option is available.

Course options/approach

Level (specify 1 for elementary, 2 for intermediate, and 3 for upper level courses.)

☐ Literature in translation _____
☐ Comparative literature _____
☐ Introduction to language/linguistics courses _____
☐ Multi-language or exploratory courses _____
☐ Intensive or accelerated courses _____
☐ Contemporary culture: taught in FL ☐ _____
                     taught in English ☐ _____
☐ Comparative cultures: taught in FL ☐ _____
                     taught in English ☐ _____
☐ Ethnic Studies: taught in FL ☐ _____
                     taught in English ☐ _____
☐ Area Studies: taught in FL ☐ _____
                     taught in English ☐ _____
☐ Immersion courses (taught in U.S.) _____
☐ Programs abroad: summer programs ☐ _____
                     academic year programs ☐ _____
☐ Special summer programs (please describe) _____

_____
_____
_____

☐ Internships for foreign language students (e.g., work in social agencies, travel bureaus, FLES teaching, undergrad. apprentice-teaching/tutoring, etc.) _____
☐ Off-campus courses (Do not include study abroad or internships.) _____
☐ Career-related courses (e.g., Scientific German, French for business majors, Spanish for medical personnel, etc.) (Do not include required courses for FL majors.) _____
☐ Community-oriented courses aimed at special non-matriculating students (e.g., foreign language for travelers, adult education courses, foreign language for children, etc.)
Please check, if such courses are offered through Division of Continuing Education rather than through your department. ☐ _____
☐ Language courses for native speakers (e.g., Spanish for Spanish-Americans) _____
☐ Special topics courses where major focus is on aspects of language or literature (e.g., genre courses; non-metropolitan literature, such as French-African, Caribbean, etc.; dialect courses; film courses; etc.) _____
☐ Special themes courses where major focus is NOT on language or literature (e.g., Women in the Hispanic World, French Cooking, etc.) _____
☐ Translation of specialized materials _____
☐ Simultaneous and/or consecutive interpretation _____

4

☐ Interdisciplinary courses
    ☐ Intra-departmental (staffed entirely within your own department)   ————
    ☐ inter-departmental (staffed by members of 2 or more departments)
☐ Critical language programs (less commonly taught languages)   ————
    Specify languages:

————————————————————————————————
————————————————————————————————

☐ Courses in which use of media is a MAJOR, INTEGRATED component.
(Do not include less commonly taught languages if available as independent
study.) Please check major medium used.   ————
    ☐ TV
    ☐ Film
    ☐ Slide/filmstrip
    ☐ Radio
    ☐ Audio-tape (including language laboratory)
    ☐ Computer-assisted instruction
    ☐ Multi-media (e.g., slide-tape)
    ☐ Other (please specify)

————————————————————————————————
————————————————————————————————

☐ Individualized instruction (Do not include less commonly taught languages if
available as independent study.)   ————
    ☐ Self-paced
    ☐ Self-instruction (audio-tutorial, independent study)
    ☐ One-to-one tutorial or small group instruction
    ☐ Mini-courses geared to special student interest
    ☐ programmed instruction
☐ Team-teaching (within department)   ————
☐ Other (please explain)   ————

————————————————————————————————
————————————————————————————————
————————————————————————————————
————————————————————————————————
————————————————————————————————

15. Does your institution or department REGULARLY administer foreign language
placement, aptitude, achievement, or attitude tests either before enrollment or
as part of a course?

Placement	Aptitude	Achievement	Attitude
☐ No	☐ No	☐ No	☐ No
☐ Yes	☐ Yes	☐ Yes	☐ Yes
	(Please specify test)		(Please specify test)
	————		————
☐ Departmental		☐ Departmental	
☐ Standardized		☐ Standardized	
(Please specify test.)		(Please specify test.)	
————		————	

5

16. Can you attribute enrollment increase OR decrease in your department to any particular factors? Consider such factors as

    a)   change in number of student contact hours per course
    b)   change in required laboratory sessions
    c)   change in number of credit hours available per course
    d)   loss or addition of faculty
    e)   budget changes
    f)   change in characteristics of student body
    g)   change in degree requirements
    h)   change in number of students fulfilling requirements through prior study or placement exam
    i)   change in general college program, etc.

Please elaborate. Continue on back of questionnaire or attach additional sheet, if necessary.

_____
_____
_____
_____
_____
_____
_____
_____
_____
_____
_____
_____
_____
_____
_____

Please return to:

Renate A. Schulz
Project Director
Foreign Language Department
State University College
Buffalo, N.Y. 14222

APPENDIX B

Numerical Analyses of Questionnaire Responses: Four-Year Colleges

Although it is diffcult to make generalizations about the data collected in the survey, an analysis of the responding sample, enrollment summaries for the commonly and less commonly taught languages, numbers of majors, and information on staffing and average course load are included in Appendix B to give readers a perspective on the responding sample and to enable them to compare their own departmental situation with that of the sample described.

Tables 1 and 2 represent a breakdown of respondents by state, type of department, size of institution, financial support (public or private), and types of degree granted. Analysis of the sample indicates that 439 (63%) of the responding departments were in small institutions (under 5,000 students); 106 departments (15%) were in medium-sized ones (5,000-10,000 students); and 148 (21%) came from large universities (over 10,000 students). The majority of responses (400 departments, or 58%) came from departments in private institutions. The B.A. or B.S. was the highest degree offered by 443 respondents (64%); 95 (14%) offered the M.A. as highest degree; and 126 (18%) offered the doctorate. Departments of foreign or modern languages accounted for 355 responses (51%); 58 (8%) came from Latin/classics departments; 51 (7%) from German departments; 19 (3%) from German/Slavic combinations; 33 (5%) from Russian/Slavic departments; and 29 (4%) from Romance language departments. In addition, 41 (6%) came from French, 27 (4%) from Spanish, and 10 (1%) from Italian departments. A very small number of responses came from departments of Scandinavian languages (4) and oriental and near-eastern languages (5); and 39 (6%) came from humanities, linguistics, departments of biblical languages, or uncommon combinations of languages such as classics and oriental languages.

TABLE I: Responding 4-Year Departments by State

State	Number of Institutions	Number of Departments	% of Total Sample
Alabama	6	6	.86
Alaska	0	0	
Arizona	2	3	.43
Arkansas	8	8	1.15
California	37	53	7.65
Colorado	8	12	1.73
Connecticut	11	17	2.45
Florida	5	5	.72
Georgia	13	16	2.31
Hawaii	2	4	.58
Idaho	3	3	.43
Illinois	19	27	3.90
Indiana	18	25	3.61
Iowa	16	19	2.74
Kansas	11	13	1.87
Kentucky	5	5	.72
Louisiana	7	9	1.30
Maine	7	7	1.01
Maryland	8	8	1.15
Massachusetts	25	39	5.63
Michigan	18	20	2.89
Minnesota	12	20	2.89
Mississippi	1	1	.14
Missouri	18	21	3.03
Montana	3	3	.43
Nebraska	7	7	1.01
Nevada	1	1	.14
New Hampshire	5	7	1.01
New Jersey	15	20	2.89
New Mexico	3	3	.43
New York	41	46	6.64
North Carolina	12	14	2.02
North Dakota	6	6	.86
Ohio	23	35	5.05
Oklahoma	8	8	1.15
Oregon	4	5	.72
Pennsylvania	41	54	7.79
Rhode Island	3	7	1.01
South Carolina	7	7	1.01
South Dakota	6	7	1.01
Tennessee	12	13	1.87
Texas	28	35	5.05
Utah	3	5	.72
Vermont	3	6	.86
Virginia	17	19	2.74
Washington	4	8	1.15
West Virginia	5	5	.72
Wisconsin	16	19	2.74
Washington, D.C.	4	8	1.15
Puerto Rico	1	1	.14
Unknown	3	3	.43
TOTAL	541	693	99.93

TABLE 2: Analysis of Responding Departments by Size of Institution, Financial Support and Highest Degree Granted

	Size of Institution				Financial Support		Highest Degree Granted			
Type of Dept.[a]	Small <5,000 students	Medium 5,000–10,000	Large over 10,000	Total	State	Private	B.A./B.S.	M.A.	Ph.D.	Other or Unknown
Foreign Lang./ Modern Lang.	260-38%	57-8%	38-5%	355-51%	155-22%	200-29%	281-41%	50-7%	13-2%	11-2%
Romance Lang.	17-2%	4-1%	8-1%	29-4%	12-2%	17-2%	14-2%	4-1%	10-1%	1
French French/Italian	18-3%	7-1%	16-2%	41-6%	17-2%	24-3%	17-2%	2	21-3%	1
Spanish Spanish/Portuguese	14-2%	6-1%	7-1%	27-4%	9-1%	18-3%	13-2%	3-.5%	10-1%	1
Italian Italian/Spanish	5-1%	2	3-1%	10-1%	3-1%	7-1%	5-1%	2	3-.5%	
German	28-4%	7-1%	16-2%	51-7%	20-3%	31-4%	24-3%	7-1%	20-3%	
German/Slavics	7-1%	3	9-1%	19-3%	12-2%	7-1%	6-1%	8-1%	5-1%	
Russian/Slavics	13-2%	7-1%	13-2%	33-5%	14-2%	19-3%	11-2%	5-1%	16-2%	1
Classics	43-6%	6-1%	9-1%	58-8%	13-2%	45-6%	38-5%	6-1%	8-1%	6-1%
Scandinavian	1		3-1%	4-1%	3-.5%	1	1		3-.5%	
Oriental (Chinese, S.E. Asian lang.)	7-1%	3	12-2%	22-3%	14-2%	8-1%	9-1%	3-.5%	10-1%	
Near Eastern Langs.	1-		4-1%	5-1%	4-1%	1	1	2	2	
Other (incl. unclassified, humanities & uncommon combinations)	25-4%	4-1%	10-1%	39-6%	17-2%	22-3%	23-3%	3-.5%	5-1%	8-1%
TOTALS	439-63%	106-15%	148-21%	693	293-42%	400-58%	443-64%	95-14%	126-18%	29-4%

[a] The number of actual programs in each language is given in Tables 3 and 4 (pp. 90 and 91).

Although many departments report an increase in enrollments between fall 1972 and fall 1976, this increase often is not proportionate with total institutional growth. Obviously, if a department increased its enrollments by 20% over the period investigated, while an institution as a whole grew 40%, the department did not attract a "fair share" of students to its offerings and, in essence, lost enrollments. One must consider, however, that departmental resources do not always permit expansion to attract a proportionate share of institutional enrollment. French at the University of California at Berkeley, for instance, reports that it cannot accommodate all interested students in lower-division language courses because of insufficient teaching personnel. The problem is especially acute in departments that have suffered cuts in faculty because of recent requirement changes. These departments are now forced to curtail their offerings regardless of student demand.

Of the 693 departments that responded, only 157 (23%) reported enrollment growth that kept up with—or surpassed—the proportionate undergraduate growth reported by the institution. The remaining 328 departments (47%) that provided departmental and institutional figures were not able to attract a proportionate share of new undergraduate enrollments.

Comparing only departmental figures between 1972 and 1976, without reference to total institutional enrollments, 247 departments (37%) reported more students in 1976 than in 1972; 3 (less than 1%) reported no change in enrollments; and 374 (54%) decreased in enrollments. Sixty-nine departments (10%) did not supply 1972/1976 figures. Table 3 presents a summary of enrollments for the six most commonly taught languages for the autumn terms of 1972 and 1976. For the total four-year period investigated, 1,577 language departments, or different language sections within departments, provided comparable figures, reporting a loss of 26,312 students (9.1%). Calculated in averages, each of the 1,577 responding language departments/sections lost an average of 16.7 students. In numerical terms, French lost the largest number of students with 14,942 losses (16.2%), followed by German with 11,414 (18.5% —the largest loss in percentage terms). In third place came Russian, reporting a loss of 1,593 students (10.8%). Latin lost 658 students (6%), and Italian dropped by 216 students (2.3%). Only Spanish reported a gain (2,511 students, or 2.5%).

TABLE 3: Total Enrollments 1972/1976: Commonly Taught Languages

Language	No. of Depts. Reporting	1972 Enrollments	1976 Enrollments	Gain/Loss + / −	% Gain/Loss
French	372	92,000	77,058	− 14,942	− 16.2
German	358	61,608	50,194	− 11,414	− 18.5
Italian	131	9,215	8,999	− 216	− 2.3
Latin	163	10,931	10,273	− 658	− 6
Russian	183	14,760	13,167	− 1,593	− 10.8
Spanish	370	100,089	102,600	+ 2,511	+ 2.5
TOTALS	1,577	288,603	262,291	− 26,312	− 9.1

A summary of enrollment changes in the less commonly taught languages is presented in Table 4. Japanese, Hawaiian, Greek, Arabic, and the Scandinavian languages showed the largest growth in numerical terms. Hebrew, Swahili, Portuguese, the less commonly taught Slavic languages, Celtic, and Basque showed losses. Altogether, the 418 departments/sections that provided figures for less commonly taught languages gained 2,526 students (14.6%) between 1972 and 1976. Most departments that offered English as a Second Language (ESL), linguistics, literature in translation, interdisciplinary studies, comparative literature, or general humanities courses also grew in enrollments.

TABLE 4: Enrollments 1972/1976—Less Commonly Taught Languages and Other Foreign Language-Related Offerings

Language	No. of Depts. Reporting	1972 Enrollments	1976 Enrollments	1972/1976 Gain/Loss	% Gain/Loss
American Indian	3	—	80	+ 80	+ 100
Arabic/Mid-Eastern Studies	27	566	973	+ 407	+ 72
Basque	1	10	6	− 4	− 40
Celtic	1	60	41	− 19	− 31.7
Chinese	44	1,163	1,201	+ 38	+ 3.3
Dutch	2	66	87	+ 21	+ 31.8
East Asian Lang./Studies	19	820	871	+ 51	+ 6.2
Esperanto	2	15	28	+ 13	+ 86.7
Gaelic	1	—	5	+ 5	+ 100
Greek	122	3,748	4,245	+ 497	+ 13.3
Hawaiian	1	563	1,100	+ 537	+ 95.4
Hebrew/Yiddish	40	870	791	− 79	− 9.1
Hungarian	1	6	10	+ 4	+ 66.7
Japanese	42	4,503	5,116	+ 613	+ 13.6
Persian/Turkish	4	84	146	+ 62	+ 73.8
Portuguese	39	1,384	1,342	− 42	− 3
Rumanian	1	—	5	+ 5	+ 100
Scandinavian Lang./Studies	20	2,586	2,951	+ 365	+ 14.1
Slavic Lang. (not including Russian)	35	562	551	− 11	− 2
Swahili	7	175	127	− 48	− 27.4
Unspecified	6	93	124	+ 31	+ 33.3
SUBTOTAL: LESS COMMONLY TAUGHT LANGUAGES	418	17,274	19,800	+ 2.526	+ 14.6
Other Foreign Language-Related Offerings:					
Classics (reported separately from Latin and Greek)	39	11,853	12,151	+ 298	+ 2.5
English as a Second Language	12	182	468	+ 286	+ 157.1
General (lit. in transl., comp. lit., interdisc., humanities courses)	24	2,247	2,498	+ 251	+ 11.2
Linguistics	16	384	826	+ 442	+ 115.1
Sign Language	1	—	175	+ 175	+ 100
SUBTOTAL: OTHER FL OFFERINGS:	92	14,666	16,118	+ 1,452	+ 9.9
TOTALS:	510	31,940	35,918	+ 3,978	+ 12.5

Figures for majors in the six most commonly taught languages were provided by 968 departments or language sections within departments. The total loss of majors between 1972 and 1976 numbered 802 (10.1%). As indicated in Table 5, which summarizes the number of graduating majors for the period investigated, French appears to have suffered the highest losses with 581 majors (19.4%). Next came German with 162 losses (12.1%) and Latin/classics with 23 (9.5%). Surprisingly, Spanish, which showed an increase in enrollments between 1972 and 1976, also showed a decrease in majors—92 or 3.2%. Only Russian and Italian indicated a gain.

TABLE 5: Departments/Sections Reporting Gains/Losses in Majors between 1972 and 1976 in Six Most Commonly Taught Languages

Language	No. of Depts./ Sections Reporting	1972 Graduating Majors	1976 Graduating Majors	1972/1976 Gain/Loss + / −	% Gain/Loss + / −
French	289	3,002	2,421	− 581	− 19.4
German	230	1,344	1,182	− 162	− 12.1
Italian	22	67	96	+ 29	+ 43.3
Latin/Classics	67	242	219	− 23	− 9.5
Russian	75	371	398	+ 27	+ 7.3
Spanish	285	2,913	2,821	− 92	− 3.2
TOTALS	968	7,939	7,137	− 802	− 10.1

Of the less commonly taught languages, 198 departments/sections reported figures for majors. Of those, 74 reported an increase in the number of majors, 33 reported no change, and 91 reported a decrease. Altogether, the less commonly taught languages reported a gain of 149 majors for the four-year period covered. These figures cannot be taken as dependable indicators of a trend. Many departments do not appear to keep records of the number of majors graduating, and some of the figures are estimates. In the less commonly taught languages a number of area studies and linguistics figures are included.

Table 6 summarizes total enrollment changes between 1972 and 1976 for all languages and offerings. Figures indicate a total loss of 22,334 students (7%).

TABLE 6: Summary of Total Enrollment Changes—1972/1976

	No. of Depts./ Sections Reporting	1972 Enrollments	1976 Enrollments	Loss/Gain − / +	% Loss/Gain
Six Most Commonly Taught Languages	1,577	288,603	262,291	− 26,312	− 9.1
Less Commonly Taught Languages	418	17,274	19,800	+ 2,526	+ 14.6
Other Foreign Language-Related Offerings	92	14,666	16,118	+ 1,452	+ 9.9
TOTALS	2,087	320,543	298,209	− 22,334	− 7

Comparing the number of undergraduate students studying foreign languages with the total number of students enrolled in undergraduate instruction reveals a slight decline in proportions over the four-year period investigated. In 1972, for example, 14.3% of all undergraduates in the survey sample studied a foreign language; in 1974 the figure had fallen to 13%, and it declined further to 12.5% in autumn of 1976, indicating a slight decrease in interest in foreign languages in general. (1974 MLA statistics report a national average of 9.9% of undergraduate enrollments studying a foreign language; see note 3 on page 78. The discrepancy between the MLA figure and that of 13% for 1974 obtained by this study confirms that we are dealing with a biased sample. A proportionately larger number of students were studying a foreign language in the responding institutions than was the case nationwide.)

The staffing patterns reflected in figures provided by questionnaires confirm what we knew already: many foreign language teaching positions have been eliminated. The 624 departments reporting comparable figures employed 5,941 full-time faculty in the fall of 1972 versus 5,504 in the fall of 1976. The total loss of teaching positions amounted to 437 (7.4%). Of the 693 respondents, 227 departments (32.8%) indicated the use of teaching assistants in undergraduate instruction. Only 198 departments provided figures for the 1972/76 period, however. For the autumn term of 1972, 2,091 T.A. positions were reported. By fall 1976, the number had decreased to 2,041, indicating a loss of 50 positions (2.4%).

Finally, the average course load carried by full-time faculty per semester or quarter could not be accurately calculated since some chairpersons reported teaching load in units or courses rather than by credit hours. Assignments ranged from 6 hours (two courses) per term to 20 hours, the mode being 12 hours and the approximate average around 11 contact hours per week.

APPENDIX C

Numerical Analyses of Questionnaire Responses: Two-Year Colleges

Table 1 presents a breakdown of two-year respondents by state. The largest number of responses came from California (19), New York, (16), Illinois (10), Michigan, Virginia (9 per state), Florida, Massachusetts, North Carolina, Texas (8 per state), Maryland, Missouri, New Jersey, and Pennsylvania (6 per state), reflecting the number and development of two-year institutions in those states.

TABLE 1: Responding Two-Year Departments by State

State	Number of Institutions Responding
Alabama	1
Arizona	2
Arkansas	3
California	19
Colorado	4
Connecticut	2
Delaware	1
Florida	8
Georgia	4
Hawaii	2
Illinois	10
Indiana	2
Iowa	3
Kansas	5
Kentucky	2
Maine	1
Maryland	6
Massachusetts	8

Michigan	9
Minnesota	1
Mississippi	1
Missouri	6
Nebraska	2
New Jersey	6
New York	16
North Carolina	8
Ohio	3
Oklahoma	2
Oregon	4
Pennsylvania	6
South Carolina	2
South Dakota	1
Tennessee	3
Texas	8
Virginia	9
Washington	5
West Virginia	1
Wisconsin	2
Wyoming	2
Location unknown	1
TOTAL	181

Only 72 of the responding departments (39.8%) were foreign language departments (or language-specific departments, such as French or Spanish). The remainder of the questionnaires came from institutions where foreign languages are taught under the auspices of umbrella departments or divisions as indicated in Table 2.

TABLE 2: Respondents from Two-Year Institutions by Type of Department

Name of Department/Division	Number Responding	%
Modern Languages, Foreign Languages, or Language-Specific	72	39.8
Humanities	41	22.7
Language Arts (English and Foreign Languages)	35	19.3
Communication or Communication and Arts	17	9.4
Liberal Arts, Cultural Arts, or Arts and Sciences	9	5
General Studies	2	1.1
Academic	1	.6
International College	1	.6
Unknown	3	1.7
TOTAL	181	100

The majority of completed questionnaires came from small (fewer than 5,000 students), publicly financed commuter colleges. Of the 181 responses, 126 (69.7) fell into the category of small institutions, 25 (13.8) were from medium-sized community colleges (5,000–10,000 students), and 17 (9.4%) were from large ones (enrollment over 10,000); 146 (80.7) of the responding institutions were publicly financed, 22 (12.2%) privately. One hundred thirty-one (72.4%) institutions were commuter colleges, and 37 (20.4%) had residential facilities. Of the remaining 13 institutions (7.2%), size, financial support, and commuter/residential status could not be determined.

TABLE 3: Languages Offered by Responding Two-Year Institutions

Languages	Number of Institutions Offering Languages	%
Spanish	158	87.3
French	154	85.1
German	109	60.2
Italian	29	16
Russian	23	12.7
Japanese	8	4.4
Chinese	7	3.9
English as a Second Language (ESL)	6	3.3
Greek	6	3.3
Hebrew	5	2.8
Latin	5	2.8
Swahili	5	2.8
Arabic	2	1.1
Pilipino	2	1.1
Swedish	2	1.1
Czech	1	.6
Finnish	1	.6
Hawaiian	1	.6
Ilocano	1	.6
Navajo	1	.6
Polish	1	.6
Portuguese	1	.6

Table 3 indicates the number of two-year colleges that offer the various languages listed. Spanish was offered most often, followed closely by French. German is available in 60% of the institutions. Italian and Russian follow far behind in popularity, offered by only 16% and 13% of the institutions respectively. Latin apparently has little appeal in two-year institutions, following Japanese, Chinese, and Greek in popularity.

Table 4 summarizes enrollment increases/decreases between the autumn terms of 1972 and 1976. Figures were reported by 433 language sections within departments.

TABLE 4: Enrollment Summary of Two-Year Institutions—1972–1976

Language	No. of Depts./ Sections Reporting	Enrollments 1972	Enrollments 1976	Loss/Gain	%
French	127	9,023	8,132	− 891	− 9.9
German	90	5,240	4,124	− 1,116	− 21.3
Italian	26	695	1,059	+ 364	+ 52.4
Russian	20	432	353	− 79	− 18.3
Spanish	134	16,608	19,240	+ 2,632	+ 15.8
Other (excluding ESL)	36	1,499	1,975	+ 476	+ 31.8
TOTALS	433	33,497	34,883	+ 1,386	+ 4.1

The responding two-year institutions experienced an overall increase in foreign language enrollments of 1,386 students (4.1%) during the four-year period investigated. Increasing enrollments were evident, however, only in Spanish

(2,632 students, or 15.8%), Italian (364 students, or 52.8%), and the less commonly taught languages, excluding Latin, Greek, and Swahili (476 students, or 31.8%). The figures in Table 4 do not include enrollments in ESL. The 6 departments reporting ESL programs showed a gain of 768 students (160%) between 1972 and 1976. French, German, and Russian showed considerable losses representing 9.9%, 21.3%, and 18.3% of the respective 1972 enrollments. German reported the greatest decline with the loss of 1,116 students.

Despite the overall foreign language enrollment increase, in the context of total 1972–1976 institutional enrollments only 22 departments (12.1%) were able to attract a proportionate or a larger number of students from the total student body at the end of the four-year period investigated; 73 institutions (40.3%) reported a decrease in students relative to total institutional enrollments; the remaining departments did not provide overall institutional enrollment figures for the periods compared.

Staffing figures were provided by 144 two-year institutions (79.6%). While these colleges reported a total of 461.06 full-time foreign language instructors in 1972, the number had shrunk to 423.03 in 1976, indicating a loss of 38.03 positions (8.2%). Fifty-eight institutions (40.3%) mentioned no change in number of foreign language faculty between 1972 and 1976, 29 (20.1%) increased the number of positions available, and 58 (40.3%) lost faculty positions. In 1972, the average number of foreign language teaching positions per institution was 3.2; in 1976 it was 2.9. The number of faculty ranged from .2 to 22 positions in both years investigated.

Finally, the average number of courses taught by full-time foreign language personnel in the two-year sample amounted to 4.1 courses, or 14.6 contact hours per week. The mode was 4 courses (15 contact hours). The number of courses ranged from 2 to 7 for full-time faculty and the number of contact hours from 9 to 25.